Second Edition
Copyright 2012 Eveline Sandy

This book remains the copyrighted property of the author, an may not be reproduced, copied and distributed for commercial or non-commercial purposes. Thank you for your support.

Eveline Sandy

"God Bless"

Eveline Sandy

Acknowledgements:

I dedicate this book to my Heavenly Father and to each and everyone who has given me the inspiration to fulfill my long-time dream.

And to the memory of my best friend and loving mother, Gertrude Behm

Eveline Sandy

Table of Contents:

ACKNOWLEDGEMENTS: 3
TABLE OF CONTENTS: 5
CHAPTER 1: MY BEGINNINGS 7
CHAPTER 2: THE FIRST MAN IN MY LIFE 11
CHAPTER 3: TO KANSAS 19
CHAPTER 4: WHERE IS MY DAD? 25
CHAPTER 5: A BAD PLACE 29
CHAPTER 6: DAD LEAVES AGAIN AND AGAIN 35
CHAPTER 7: MY PARTNER IN CRIME 39
CHAPTER 8: BELOIT 43
CHAPTER 9: OFF TO GRANDPARENT'S HOUSE WE GO 53
CHAPTER 10: MOM, MY PILLAR 55
CHAPTER 11: HE'S NOT COMING BACK 59
CHAPTER 12: A SIGHT FOR SORE EYES 65
CHAPTER 13: A MIRACLE HAPPENS 67
CHAPTER 14: MY WORLD CRASHES AROUND ME 73
CHAPTER 15: MY UNCLE'S INSIGHT 77
CHAPTER 16: MY DEAREST FRIENDS 81
CHAPTER 17: FIRST LOVE 87
CHAPTER 18: GRADUATION 91
CHAPTER 19: MY ISLAND TRIP 93
CHAPTER 20: REALITY CHECK 95
CHAPTER 21: PHILLIP 97
CHAPTER 22: LIFE DECISION 101
CHAPTER 23: ENTER CHRISTOPHER THOMAS 107
CHAPTER 24: LIFE GOES ON. 111
CHAPTER 25: HOME BASED IN PHOENIX 117
CHAPTER 26: DONALD SANDY - MY MAN FOR LIFE 119
CHAPTER 27: ENTER JESSE LEE SANDY 131
CHAPTER 28: MOM IS LOSING THE BATTLE 143
EPILOGUE: 159
READERS SAY: 163
ABOUT THE AUTHOR: 169
OUR VISION 173

Eveline Sandy

Chapter 1: My Beginnings

"*Mein Liebchen.*" Although my mother named me Eveline, this is the name I most remember her using. My loved one.

I was born on January 7, 1958 in the quaint town of Karlsrhue, in western Germany.

Karlsruhe, Germany

My mother's name was Gertrude, but everyone called her Susie. She was twenty-years-old and unmarried when I was born. She had met an American soldier who promised her everything, but left her with just one thing, a daughter who weighed only four pounds at birth.

My mother was a beautiful woman; small and graceful. She had wavy, blonde hair and blue eyes that sparkled. Her light complexion was soft and smooth. When she walked, it seemed like she was floating.

In every way, my mother was a lady. She loved to dress up, adding matching shoes and purses, which were her special weakness. She often wore bright, happy colors that reflected her personality. She had two lovely babushkas, which are German scarves, that she wore when she went out.

Mother learned English by watching television and listening to American music. Her favorite song was "White Christmas." She never cussed in German or English. She didn't think it was ladylike.

When my mother very young, my Grandfather Herr Behm went to prison for beating my Grandmother, Emma Behm. He was a very abusive man to both my *Grossmutter* (Grandmother) and *Mutter* (Mother).

Even though it was a relief for everyone when Grandfather went to prison, it didn't make the situation any easier as far as food and money for my German family. My mother, along with the remaining family, was very, very poor during the war era. The family lived on the East side of the Berlin Wall, and everything was extremely scarce and rationed out. When my Grandfather was released from prison, he went to fight in the war and was killed in action.

During this time, the East side of Germany was controlled by the Russians, and there was very little freedom and a lot of rules. After the war, the West side was "occupied" by the U.S., France and Great Britain, and boasted freedom and jobs and less rationing. Between 1954 and 1960 many professionals, doctors, lawyers, teachers ,etc., moved from the East side to the West side.

Traveling back and forth between the two sides, prior to 1961, was easy and not very restricted. In 1946, when she was only fourteen-years-old, Mom started traveling between the two sides. Her family accepted her traveling, knowing Mom's deep desire for freedom.

Then in 1961 some brilliant person decided that "The Berlin Wall" was to be built. It came with many restrictions and much less contact between the two sides. Crossing over was extremely restricted. Bravely, for one last time, she traveled alone to the west side of Germany on a train, to live there permanently. Her contact with her family was virtually cut off.

Obviously, Mom needed a job because she didn't bring much money with her when she left home. Luckily, she was able to get a job right away. She became a nanny for a prominent doctor's family. She lived in their home so she didn't have to worry about shelter or food. She loved the doctor's children and got plenty of practice with the little ones.

Life was better, simply because there were no more beatings to endure, and Mom had the freedom to make her own choices.

Although there were still long lines to wait for food, and there were shortages of most items due to the war, it was much worse on the East side of Germany. Still, the freedom was rich and satisfying. No more looking over her shoulder, and no more fear of governmental punishment. No more sirens and air raids. But she was to learn that freedom always has a price.

Eveline Sandy

Chapter 2: The First Man in My Life

When I was two years old, my father came into our lives. It wasn't until years later that I learned the truth, that the man I called Dad was not my birth father. His name was Michael, and he was 5"10' with a stocky build and dark hair. He was in the United States Army and stationed in a town not far from where Mom worked. It was called Sindelfingen, Germany.

Dad didn't speak a lot of German, and Mom didn't speak any English. Somehow they communicated with gestures and smiles. They were truly in love with each other, or at least in the beginning Dad was. There was never another man in my mother's life that she truly loved and was devoted to as much as him. I can't say the same faithfulness was in Dad for Mom.

Sometimes I wondered how Mom could continue to love him and give Dad total devotion, and he could still cheat on her and lie to her.

Although, I didn't feel it was right, Mom taught me a valuable lifelong lesson. It's called unconditional love. It is best described in the Bible:

> *1Corinthians13:4-8*
> *"Love is patient, love is kind. It does not envy, it does not boast, it is not proud. It is not rude, it is not self-seeking. It is not easily angered; it keeps no record of wrongs. Love does not delight in evil but rejoices with the truth. It always protects, always trusts, always hopes, and always perseveres. Love never fails..."*

I believe, totally, if we all followed those Godly words, we would all be fulfilling the Lord's directive of "love thy neighbor as thy self."

Mom read her Bible every day. She was raised in the Protestant religion. Dad didn't encourage us to attend church services. Mom's idea was a family goes places together, whether it's church or shopping. Mom told me quietly about God when Dad wasn't around. She taught me some prayers in German that I have passed down to my children and grandchildren. One of my favorite prayers that we said every night before I fell asleep was in German:

*"Ich bin wenig
Mein Herz ist rein
Sagen, der Herr uber
Und Jesus allein
Amen."*

I'll translate it:

*"I am little,
My heart is pure
To the Lord above,
And to Jesus Alone,
Amen"*

And then Mom would say in German, as she tucked me in, *"Schlaf gut mit Gott"* "Sleep good with God."

Mom never tore me down. She never spanked me. She always tried to understand why I did things the way I chose to do them. She discussed my choices, good and bad, with me. She never judged me. She guided me with suggestions. Sometimes, I could see the sadness in her eyes because of the situations I would get into.

I think that's why there were some things I couldn't tell her, because she would be so terribly disappointed in me. I couldn't bear to see her eyes filled with sadness. Mom always believed in people and that they were basically good. That belief stayed with her, throughout her entire life. It is my belief now, as well.

My Mother and I

Dad could be like a drill sergeant most of the time, and wanted life to be spit-spot and have it his way in all things. During this time we went through the usual adjustments for a blended-race family, with the added stress of the language barrier. We were all very happy though, because love can overcome most difficulties.

Within a relatively short time after the wedding, Dad got transfer orders to return back to the States. He brought Mom and me with him, and we moved to El Paso, Texas.

We were on a ship starting out on June 14, 1957, traveling to the States. The trip took eleven days.

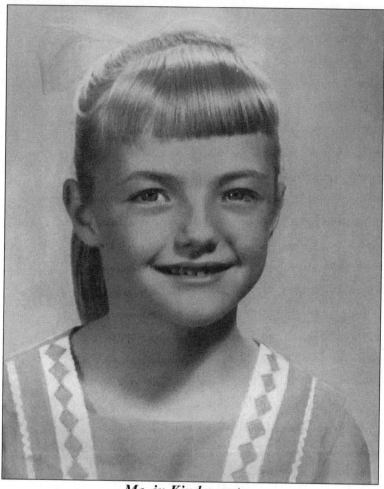

Me, in Kindergarten

The endless up and down motion of the ship made the trip seem forever. There was water; water everywhere. Before we embarked on this journey, Mom received letter after letter from my German grandmother begging her to let me remain and be raised by my grandmother.

Grossmutter maintained that if I stayed with her, my mother would surely return to Germany for me and ultimately stay with the family. Unfortunately, Mom didn't agree and took me with her. Perhaps Dad had an influence in this. All I know is Mom never returned to Germany to see her mom and family ever again.

After we landed at Ellis Island in New York we went to Dad's assigned base, which was in Texas. We were in El Paso, for such a short time, and it was uneventful as far as my memory of it goes. Nothing comes to mind, except my Mom tried to learn to drive. She drove the car down the driveway, stalled and then drove right back into the garage. She said she didn't want to drive anymore, so she never did again.

I can't imagine how Mom dealt with coming to a strange country, not really knowing the language and not always sure Dad would be there as he should have. I can appreciate all the effort she put into raising me in this strange land and providing me with freedom.

Shortly after, Dad got transfer orders back to Germany. Again, he took us with him. We moved an awful lot during my childhood. I guess that's where the term "Army Brats" comes from.

We were always moving around, always readjusting to our surroundings. We lived in Germany until I was to go to first grade, then we moved back to the States again.

This time, we lived off base in Junction City, Kansas, which is just outside of Fort Riley, Kansas, where he reported for duty. I didn't speak any English when I started first grade in the States, even though I was a little German chatterbox.

It was a bit of a challenge for me. I had a tutor daily in school, and I still couldn't understand anyone. I eventually put bits and pieces together. It took me about two years to learn English. Mom taught me excellent German from the time I could talk.

German is such a pretty language. I had a very heavy German accent until I was in sixth grade. Today, I speak both English and German equally and have no trace of a German accent in my English.

I was fearful hearing all the other school children speak English. I thought they were making fun of me. Soon, I learned everyone was trying to be nice to me. My mother was very helpful in my language learning process. She told me I could speak German at home but in public it had to be English. She felt very strongly about this.

It wasn't easy for Mom, not knowing much English. I was her translator and often spoke for her to other people.

Mom told me stories about our family in Germany and events during her growing up years. I could listen for hours about the surroundings and her description of our relations and the food they ate.

We didn't have much food during my growing up years but with what we did have, Mom would prepare tasty meals. She made German potato salad, fried potatoes and onions, sauerkraut, bratwurst, schnitzels, and pork chops, German style. She made a macaroni and hamburger casserole I still make today. She didn't have any recipes written down, so she prepared it all from memory. My mouth is watering with the memory of her home cooked meals.

Sometimes I would look at Mom and she would have a yearning in her eyes. She wanted deeply to return to Germany someday and see her family again. It was a great burden she carried, knowing she never could because of lack of money for such a trip. She was barely surviving here in America. Sometimes I compared her to the mermaid looking out to sea, never to return.

Christmastime was especially rough on Mom. Sometimes, I could hear her crying in her bedroom softly moaning: "*Mama, mama Ich wunschte, wir waren zusammen.*" "Mama, mama, I wish we were together."

Mom's mama died in 1997. They never saw each other again after Mom left home in the '50's.

In later years, when I visited my aunts and uncles in Germany I was fearful I forgot how to speak my native tongue and wouldn't be able to converse with my *gross mutter* (grandmother). I prayed and prayed about my fears to the Lord. And the Lord answered me in a dream:

"*Kind warum sollte ich Ihnen nach Hause, wenn Sie nicht zu ihrer Grossmutter zu redden?*" "Child, why would I send you home, if you couldn't speak to your grandmother?"

My Grandmother

Truly, the Lord answers all prayers. I speak with them fairly regularly now by phone and computer. It has finally put my soul at peace that I have family continuity. I never was exposed to the true essence of family interaction; now I cherish it.

Eveline Sandy

Chapter 3: To Kansas

All three of us lived in a compact two bedroom, one bath trailer. It was nice. Dad seemed to be home a lot more than before. It didn't last for long, because Dad had to leave and go back to the war. This didn't really make any sense to me when he had to leave.

Dad said he had to go, and off he went. Dad was gone a long, long time, and I really missed him. We didn't have a lot of money, but we always seemed to make it somehow.

At first, Dad sent us money regularly. Then, gradually the money stopped coming. The military, in those days, didn't make the servicemen support the families they left behind. Mom wrote letter after letter to Dad asking for help, but he didn't respond back. She finally wrote a letter to his commanding officer. That didn't work either. Mom had no choice but to go to work or we would be homeless and without food.

My Mom was always there for me. We always had a roof over our heads and food on the table. I guess it was easier on Mom having only one child to be worried about. She wouldn't let life get her down. She taught me to think the same way.

Barton's Grocery Store was across the road from my school. Mom would give me a food list in German, then I would go to the store after school and shop for us. We didn't have the money for food so we would run a monthly tab with Mr. Barton. He would then forgive any debt we had at the end of the month and tear up our bill. He was a very kind and generous man. I don't know what we would have done without him.

Mom finally found a job as a waitress at a local restaurant and bar. I knew it wasn't easy for her because she didn't speak much English. The other waitresses helped her if she couldn't understand a customer. They were all very kind to her.

I remember Dad and Mom taking time off to go and visit Dad's parents, my grandmother, Alice, and grandfather, Able. My grandparents loved me so, especially Grandpa. He liked taking me places, and we always stopped at the local ice cream parlor for ice cream cones. Also, when we went to Aunt Laura's in Delta, Ohio, we would stop on the way for ice cream. I can remember when Aunt Laura only had my cousin Ricky. She and Ricky lived in the bottom half of her home. She rented out the top half to help her pay the bills.

My grandparents lived in Bettsville, Ohio which was about one hour away from Aunt Laura's house. They had lived there since I was very small. Lucky for them, they didn't move around like we did. We all got along so very well, and my grandparents thought a lot of me, as well as Mom, even considering we weren't blood relations. I was too small to know the difference anyway.

Throughout my life my father consistently asked me to lie for him. On one occasion I remember my dad called my grandparents and lied to them by saying I desperately needed an operation, and we didn't have the money for it. Could they please send him money?

Then, when they hesitated, he would make me get on the phone, pinch me first to get me to cry and then ask for help from them. They agreed immediately, because they wouldn't allow their granddaughter to suffer needlessly.

I never needed an operation and I don't know why my father always had to lie to get things. When they sent him the money for my "operation" he took their money to buy a car with it. His parents never found out the truth that I know of.

As far as my mom is concerned, my Dad would threaten her if she wouldn't agree to these lies. My dad controlled my mother to such a degree that she was forbidden to tell anyone the truth of what was going on in the household.

When my dad came back from the war; this time from Korea, his attitude had really changed a lot. He was constantly drinking and did not want to be around Mom as much as before. I remember he used to hit her when he was drunk. He never hit me though.

I know it affected her to do this. She was brought up to be truthful and honorable. She wanted to verbalize her feelings and couldn't. She was afraid she would be thrown out, along with me. She was in a strange country and a different culture with a man that was unethical and dishonest.

Mom kept an eye on me so Dad wouldn't take out his anger on me. He never did hit me, and I can thank Mom for that. She was my champion at her own expense.

I used to cry a lot because I didn't understand what the problem was. I loved both Mom and Dad and felt very torn. I hoped and prayed things would be better in time. I used to always hear the adults say that, so I had to believe it.

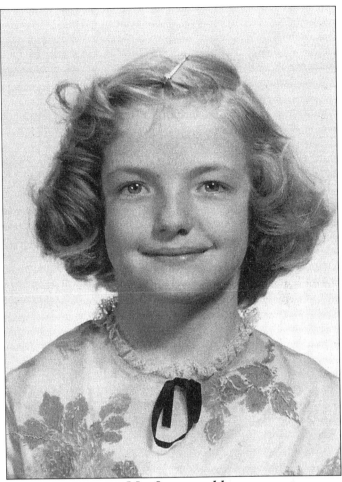

Me, 9 years old

    I can't tell you enough how much children feel abandoned, torn and fearful when there is discord between their parents. It is like a child's security has been ripped away. There are so many broken homes out there, and broken hearts that include the children. They are truly the innocent victims. Never involve your children in your differences with your spouse, and please don't use them as your pawns. The children feel pushed and pulled as it is.

    Things didn't get better between my Mom and Dad. It seemed Dad cared about me, but not about my Mom anymore. He started going out with other women.

I would see it and then tell Mom, but Mom would never believe me. She would respond by saying, "No, your dad loves me so. Your dad works hard, and it just seems like he's gone all the time." She just wouldn't accept any other explanation.

My nature was not to worry about most things, nevertheless it was hard to actually see my Dad with a woman that wasn't my Mom. It was very confusing, because I really didn't understand, and then I wondered why. I started believing that maybe I did something wrong. All that conflict bottled up in one small child is confusing.

If I needed something for school, Dad would always get it for me. If Mom needed anything, no matter how necessary, Dad would always refuse her. It wasn't fair! My mom loved him through and through, and he was the only man, the only husband, for her whole life. She had such loyalty, commitment, and unconditional love!

I do have to say that my dad was instrumental in my maintaining school discipline and keeping up good grades. In many ways, his military style and rules would show at home. If I didn't understand some subject he would drill it into me, not mean-like, but consistently.

Sometimes he would have me stay up at the kitchen table going over and over and over the subject matter until I got it right. Sometimes that would be until midnight. It wasn't fun, but by golly, I learned to be persistent with my studies until I knew what I was doing.

One day, I asked Mom if I could spend the night with a girlfriend. Mom didn't really like me away from home overnight, but she finally said alright. I was so excited! I had packed everything I thought I might need earlier in the day. Finally the time came to go to my friend's home. I was having a great time with her until a knock came to the door. My girlfriend Pat said, "Eve would you answer the door?"

I said "Sure," and off to the door I went. As I opened the door, I was stunned to see my father standing there. He was holding a small gift-wrapped box in his hand. It wasn't for me. But, if it wasn't for me, who was it for?

I wanted to run and hide and not talk to anyone. My dad didn't say much except that he got a watch for Pat's mom and not to tell my Mom. My Dad was "seeing" my friend's mom.

Eventually my Dad left. I stayed overnight as planned, and Pat and I talked an awful lot about the situation but nothing made much sense to me.

My Dad gave Pat's mom a diamond watch as a gift. Pretty good, huh? He never could afford to buy Mom anything nice or even the necessities.

I went home the next day, telling Mom I had a wonderful time and hoped she didn't miss me very much; I know she did though. I kept quiet for awhile but I couldn't hold the watch business in anymore. I loved my mom so very much. I didn't want to see her hurt. I wanted us all together. If she realized what my Dad was doing, I knew Mom would try and fix it.

So, I told Mom what had happened about the watch and Dad. I told her everything that I knew. I didn't promise Dad I wouldn't tell either. It was too much for me to carry inside me.

Mom didn't believe a word I said to her. She said my eight-year-old brain worked overtime. I just couldn't think of how to convince her of the truth. I don't think she wanted to accept it.

When Mom got her jewelry bill the following month she couldn't figure out how a diamond watch was charged on the bill. She called the jewelers and was told Dad bought it. Well, Mom didn't have a gift from Dad, so where was this diamond watch?

When Dad got home she confronted him and let him have it. They fought for days, but to me it seemed like weeks. Dad lied and wouldn't tell her the truth, and he didn't ask for forgiveness either.

After that they went through a period of not talking to each other at all. Those days were not very happy for me. When Dad would go to work Mom would cry all day because she was so sad. She was trying not to believe her husband was cheating on her.

After a while, Mom swallowed her pride; they made up, and we were back together as a happy family again. I finally could feel happy, too. Dad was nice again and took us places like he did before. It seemed like I was living on a bouncing ball, either feeling up or down.

Eveline Sandy

Chapter 4: Where is my Dad?

School was great, I always loved it. School not only gave Mom a break from me, but I enjoyed learning and seeing her face light up when I brought home my report card. I had excellent grades. I can attribute that to Dad's discipline on homework. He would always buy me little, inexpensive things to reward my good grades.

Even though we didn't have a lot, Mom and Dad bought me a dog, a Pekingese, that I called Bootsie Bubbles. What a name for a dog.

As Bootsie grew older, he knew when I was coming home from school. It was neat. He would bark at the door awaiting my arrival. We were really inseparable. Bootsie would follow me all around our home. I would put on my record player, and invite all my friends over to dance, and here was Bootsie "dancing" right along with us. It was a blast!

We did get one other dog, a Chihuahua named Pinky. She was more Mom's dog. Don't get me wrong she was cute and all, but Bootsie was all mine.

Then one day, Dad came home and said we had to move out of our trailer. Was I ever sad. He also said we would have to get rid of Bootsie and Pinky. I began crying and crying because I would never see Bootsie again. I was tired of moving around and losing things. Now I would lose my beloved pet, too.

I don't remember having a favorite toy or blanket. I wasn't much into dolls; I was a tomboy. Bootsie meant everything to me. Bootsie even slept with me at night. Bootsie would wake me up in the morning by licking my face until there was nothing I could do but get up. To this day, I don't know what my Dad did with my dogs, but I will never forget Bootsie.

We went back to stay with my grandma and grandpa again and lived there for a while. Dad wouldn't allow me to bring my pets to Grandpa's house or farm. I am not sure why. I again had to transfer to a new school. That part was okay, because I already knew most of the kids in the neighborhood.

Grandpa had a farm on the outskirts of town and a house in town. We lived in the house. The guy next door was a barber, and there was a family by the name of Coato who lived on the other side of my grandparents.

At the farm I can remember all the types of animals there. There were chickens, horses, cows, goats and a couple of pigs. Grandpa also had corn planted, and he let me shuck the corn for fun.

When Grandpa brought the chicken's home, my job was to keep an eye on them because they were having babies, and it wasn't safe for them at the farm. It was neat getting up every morning and running out to see how the chickens were. I had a fun time on the farm.

After about three weeks, Dad re-enlisted and was gone again, off to war. Now it was just Mom and me staying with my grandparents. Mom didn't really want to stay there, but did it for Dad, because he knew that we would be alright there. He figured if he didn't send any money to us, my grandparents would take care of us, because they loved us as their own. Apparently, Dad didn't have any intentions of sending money to Mom for our support.

I can recall when my grandfather sat down and asked my Mom what had "gotten into" my father, because he had changed so much. He wasn't making good choices.

Mom said it was the war causing all the bad things my dad was doing. She told Grandpa she loved Dad, very much. Even when my grandparents talked bad about their son, my Mom defended him.

Dad's re-enlistment took him back to Viet Nam. Now, I wonder if he re-enlisted to escape from the responsibilities of being a husband and father. I thought the last time he was gone was a long, long time, but each time he left it was for longer and longer periods. Mom didn't seem happy anymore. She would get pretty quiet, sitting and thinking about Dad.

I recall, Mom got a package from Dad. It was of a roll of blue and a roll of red, silky material threaded with gold inlay. Several years later I designed and sewed a dress for Mom out of the red material. She looked beautiful in it. I still have my bolt of the beautiful blue, silk material today.

When she didn't get any letters from Dad, she would worry, wondering if he had been shot, or even if he was still alive. In those days a lot of people had sons, husbands, relatives and friends off at war. It must have been just as hard for them as it was for us. I could relate with a lot of them.

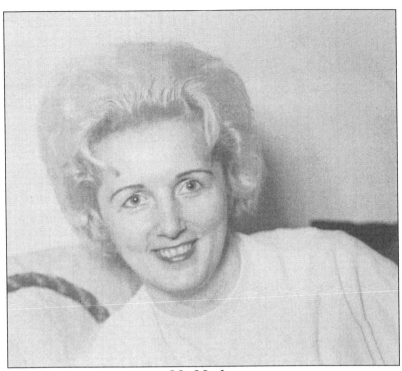

My Mother

Eveline Sandy

Chapter 5: A Bad Place

It was during that time when something happened that would affect me for the rest of my life. The evening started out with a bunch of us friends wanting to go to the drive-in theater to see a current show.

We all were young; I was only a few months past twelve, and one of our older friends drove. This didn't happen very often; it was a special treat. We were all in agreement that it was great fun to go to the drive-in!

I asked Mom if I could go, and she said okay, and to be home by a certain time. We all met up at Darlene's house, and then we were on our way for a great evening, laughing, smiling and carrying on as young girls can.

The weather was perfect for a drive-in movie. It was a warm, spring evening, not hot, not cold, but just right. We drove around and found the spot we wanted, parked and got our blankets out to sit on the ground since it was so nice out.

Halfway through the show I told my friends I needed to use the girl's room. They offered to go with me, but I said I was okay to go alone.

My stomach was upset, probably because I ate too much popcorn and candy, and I was feeling very nauseated. It wasn't a long walk, although the bathroom was set off by itself from the main building. It was well lit, and I remember there weren't a lot of people around.

I went inside hoping my stomach would feel better. I finished washing my hands and headed out the door. To my surprise there was a strange guy outside the door, waiting and looking at me. I started feeling afraid; all I wanted, was to get back to my friends. That never happened.

Suddenly, this guy grabbed my arm and threw me into a nearby parked car that I hadn't noticed before. I wanted to scream so loud, but it happened so fast. They tied a gag around my mouth to stop me from screaming.

My heart was racing, and I was scared to death. There were three other guys in the car; two in the front and one in the backseat. All I could remember is thinking, "What did I do wrong now? I just went to the bathroom like everyone else would do, but look what happened to me."

I was whimpering and sobbing because I was so scared. They shouted at me to be quiet and not say a word if I knew what was best for me. I was shaking like a leaf, not knowing what would happen next. It was a nightmare I thought would never end.

These guys drove it seemed, for a long, long time out of town. Maybe it wasn't that far away, but as scared as I was, minutes seemed like hours. I tried looking out the window, and one of the guys yanked my head back down. I was totally lost at this point. I wanted my Mom desperately to help me, but there wasn't anyone who could help me.

Finally the vehicle stopped, and I looked up and saw a big, open field with nothing else around for miles. It was dark, so I really couldn't make out any structures, or anything else. There weren't any lights either.

Two of the guys in the back of the car pulled my clothes off. I was lying there shivering with fear and naked. I couldn't stop my sobbing. The guys were all laughing, thinking this whole thing was funny. I was never naked in front of a guy before. I was a virgin, and I didn't know what was going to happen next.

They were talking, and I heard them say, "We have a real young one here, that's the best kind!" The way they talked it was like they did this before. At that point I didn't know what that comment implied, but I was about to find out.

What was going to happen to me? I prayed silently in my mind, like Mom forever told me to do when things seemed their hardest. I think my brain shut down so I wouldn't have to feel and think about what they were doing to me.

That night, at twelve years old, I lost my virginity, not by choice or design. Not by one male but by four vicious, unfeeling males.

When they were done with me I pleaded for them to drop me off somewhere, I didn't care where. I promised I wouldn't say a word to anyone about what happened. That didn't work.

The first guy grabbed me and shoved me down and roughly re-entered me. I was sobbing; I hadn't stopped crying since they took me. I didn't know I had that many tears in me. I remember him saying, "Who's next?" They were like a bunch of animals. The next guy was not as big as the first guy but he was nasty smelling. They all smelled bad. They must have been drinking a lot. I never in my life thought this would happen to me.

One of the guys held a gun to my head and said, "Don't move if you know what's best, b***h."

I couldn't move anyway because I was so sore and scared. God, I wanted my Mom. The one in the front seat got out and climbed on top of me in the back seat. All the others were outside the car. I heard one of them say, "Wow, what a good time boys, we won't forget this!"

As they were laughing and playing it up, I kept thinking, "What about me?" They didn't realize, nor care, that I also would not forget this in my lifetime. They destroyed a part of me that I will never get back. It was terrible nightmare and then the fourth one was screaming at me, saying terrible things to me and calling me horrible names. Most of the time they kept saying things like, "Don't tell your mother or father, you bitch, or we will kill them and you. And don't go to the police because you can't prove a thing." I was so afraid they would kill me or my parents.

They finally got done with what they wanted to do with me. I lay there bleeding, filthy, bruised and sore; in shock and disbelief. I kept pleading over and over again, "What did I do to deserve this? What did I do wrong?" They responded laughingly, "If it wasn't you Bitch it would be someone else. We wanted to gang-rape someone. It's your problem that you were such an easy target."

They all got back in the car, shoved me in the corner of the back seat and drove down Main Street in the center of town. They slowed, opened the back door and tossed me out like old garbage. I tucked myself as best I could and rolled onto the street with no clothing on.

There was no one around, and I lay still for a few moments, then I got myself up and tried to concentrate so I could figure out where I was. For a few blocks I was running, and then I recognized a small house close to where we lived on Main Street.

A wonderful, kind lady lived there that both Mom and I knew. I banged on the door a few times, and she finally came and opened it. She started crying when she saw me. She gently asked, "What happened to you, little one?"

All I could do was sob, "You won't believe it, because I can't believe it!" As she took me inside her home and put a blanket around me, all I could do was repeat over and over, "Please don't tell Mom." After a time she agreed.

I told the little old lady everything I could remember. She did call my mom at work and told her I got sick at the drive in and she would let me stay at her home until tomorrow. Mom said it would be alright because she liked the lady so much and trusted her. I started crying again. I felt so filthy and dirty and degraded.

This wonderful lady filled the wash tub with soothing, warm water and told me to get in and soak for awhile, and it would help me feel better. I asked her for a bath brush, and she went and got me one.

She left me alone, and as I sat there I just kept scrubbing and scrubbing. I was trying to scrub the pain away and the memories that caused the pain. The horrible events kept running through my mind over and over again. To this day, every detail is still vivid as if it just happened.

I believe one day, if it hasn't happened already that these men will pay for what they did to me. "God's mill grinds slow but sure" is a true expression. I know God will and already has punished them. They will answer for taking my childhood away and the opportunity of being a virgin on my wedding day.

Finally, I finished bathing, and this kind lady came in and invited me to sit on the sofa with her. So I did, and she held me in her arms and told me everything would be alright. I just sat there accepting her warm embrace and comforting words. Inside, there didn't seem anything left I could share. I felt so alone.

I really wanted to tell my wonderful mother what happened to me, and I knew she would gather me up in her loving arms, but I just couldn't. I truly believed if I told her and she tried to do anything, those awful men would kill her. I couldn't bear losing my mother. Mom was my whole world, and I needed to protect her right now. She had been through enough herself. I didn't want to add another burden to carry on her small shoulders.

I just sat with the kind lady and cried and cried. I finally fell asleep and just didn't want to wake up and think about this anymore. Morning came and the physical pain, as well as the emotional pain, was still there. My whole outlook on men changed from that point forward.

It was time to go back home. I thanked the kind lady and left. She had given me some clothes to wear, and luckily my mom didn't ask me about them. I ran to the bathroom and changed and came out to greet my mom.

Seeing my Mom was the greatest sight ever. I loved her so much and knew it wasn't going to be easy keeping this secret from her. We usually shared everything between us. There wasn't too much I couldn't tell her about my life except this.

I never saw those terrible boys again. I don't know what town they lived in or worked, or where they went to school. Thank God for that. There were many times I wish I could have done something about my rape, but every time I thought I had the guts to I thought about them threatening to kill my Mom.

I'm so lucky I didn't get pregnant, or get any diseases from them, or permanent physical damage. As far as emotional damage, it was permanent and never goes away. It affected my self-esteem in future relationships. I will always walk around with a deep hurt inside. I didn't have any counseling; I didn't have anyone to talk through this fear of males that still remains with me.

Me, Age 12

Eveline Sandy

Chapter 6: Dad Leaves Again and Again

Mom and I found out Dad was okay while he was in 'Nam'. He finally sent a letter to Mom. Thank God; although the war changed him a lot. Dad finally came home again; oh boy! We now all lived together for a short time at my grandparent's home. What fun to have him back in our lives!

One day we traveled to our old home town and visited some of our old friends. Before we left to go back to my grandparents, Dad really seemed sorry about his friends that he found out had died in the war.

Dad did some strange things while we lived at my grandparents. My dad gave one of his friends $50.00 to go out to dinner. Mom seemed pretty surprised about that. We really didn't have the money to be handing out to everyone. Mom just smiled when Dad did it. A few days later, we moved away.

Everything seemed just fine all the way back to Junction City, Kansas. Dad was joking and laughing with Mom and myself. He hugged us and told us how much he loved us. I was glad to be home again. We were so happy as a family. Mom finally started to have a smiling personality again and stopped being depressed all the time.

It was overdue for her. Mom was very special, with a warm, wonderful and very understanding way about her. There I go again, I adored her!

Well, we got all settled in, and Dad started drinking again, as before. He could never just be happy with life as it was. Mom would try to overlook his behavior most of the time.

Then there were times when she thought if she would join him in drinking, he wouldn't get so angry at life in general. She did try to be a social drinker, but she really didn't like the feeling.

We were living in the small trailer again, and Mom would always keep an eye on me to make sure I went to bed on time. I would lie in bed and wonder if everything would ever be okay again. There were times when Dad would come home drunk and start hollering and screaming at Mom.

I would cower in bed and cry until I fell asleep. I worried; wondering if I did something wrong, to have him holler so much at Mom.

He would tell us stories about his friends who were shot, or blown to pieces, and we would sit and listen to him. As you can imagine, we couldn't relate. We hadn't experienced the horrors of war. It must have been extremely hard for Dad to think about the war and experience all that death around him. Maybe that's why Mom was so forgiving of him, because she lived in a war zone.

Dad was home for about two years, and then it was time to go back to the war again. I thought for sure my Mom just wouldn't take it anymore. She didn't know what to do or where to go; she was very confused.

Dad told her everything would be alright, and it wouldn't be long before he would be home again. This time Dad said, "I left enough meat in the freezer to keep you two fed for months and months. No worries."

As we both kissed him goodbye, Mom seemed so sad. She had that look on her face that seemed to say, "Will I ever see him again?"

We went back into the house, Mom looked in the freezer and guess what? There wasn't any meat. Dad had filled the freezer with bones!

We don't know why he lied. It wasn't a matter of not understanding what he said. Mom was really hurt. I wondered if he really and truly cared about us. Mom and I had been through a lot, but this sure took the cake.

Again, my Dad didn't send us any money to live on. I remember Mom taking all the jewelry Dad had sent from overseas and pawning it so we would have money to eat on. She loved the jewelry, especially because Dad had given it to her, and it broke her heart, but she had no choice but to pawn it. She had every intention to redeem the jewelry, but there was never extra money, so she lost it all.

If only Dad had sent us money to live on. It didn't feel like he took care of us and like he didn't want us anymore. What makes a person so irresponsible?

We had no choice, but to move out of the trailer. We moved into a tiny apartment above a house an elderly couple owned. It was okay. It had one bedroom that Mom and I shared. Mom won a stereo and a sewing machine from a radio station. She loved those prizes. Eventually, she also had to sell them to provide money for us to eat. I cannot describe how hard it was in those days.

Mom had to go to work, but she was limited on the types of jobs, because of her lack of understanding the English language. It didn't come easy to her.

She did find a job as a waitress again. The other waitresses helped Mom with English and with giving change and such things. This time she had to work evenings, which was hard on me because I was alone at night.

I used to go down to where she worked and get some money from her to go to the movie show. I met a girlfriend at school; her name was Jeaneen. We went everywhere together.

Jeaneen came from a large family. Jeaneen's father didn't like us hanging around together, because she wouldn't be available to watch her younger brothers and sisters. Her father expected her to baby-sit all the time she wasn't in school, which left little time for us. All Jeaneen wanted was to have a normal kid's fun-time once in a while and not be always babysitting for her brothers and sisters.

I remember one time when Mom got off of work at night and one of her friends walked her home. As soon as they got to the top of the stairs, they saw the door was open. Mom thought I was home and as soon as she entered the apartment, she saw everything was a mess. The person who was with her went into the living room and looked into the hall closet and discovered a man hiding in the corner.

They called the police, and he was hauled away. The police said the prowler was crazy and escaped from the mental institution nearby. Luckily, I wasn't home. Mom went over and stayed at her friend, Hazel's, apartment.

In the meantime I went home, and Jeaneen stayed over with me that night. Mom left me a note explaining what happened and wanted me to go where she was. I chose not to go, but I couldn't let Mom know because there wasn't a phone in the apartment. Jeaneen and I opened the living room windows and sat out on the roof to see the cars go by and people passing. We got so good, we could name the make and model of each car.

The next day, I had to go to Hazel's apartment where my Mom was. We moved from the previous apartment, because it was too expensive for us to live there anymore.

So, now we moved into a studio that belonged to Hazel. I guess that's what you called one big room to live in. We had a kitchen, living area and bed area combined. It was very teeny. The bathroom was in the main house.

Hazel was the lady who rented out the apartment and rooms in the second floor of her huge home. It was okay, but I couldn't wait for Dad to come back home again. It just seemed so empty without him around. Dad would write every once in a while, not too often.

It seemed very hard for Mom, being alone. I know she had me by her side at all times, but another adult to make decisions with was essential.

Mom was married, but because Dad wasn't around she didn't have his emotional support as a husband. I used to wonder how Mom really felt, watching other married people laugh and go places together. It must have torn her up. When she was in her "down" time all she said was, "*Ich will nachhause gehen*," "I want to go home," "*Ich will meine Mama wieder sehen*." "I want to see my mom again."

I would tell her to go out and have a good time because she really deserved it. Once in a while she would, and then feel guilty about it later. Mom would always tell me that in time, things would get a lot better! I would always wonder when that elusive day would get here. I loved Mom so much, that I chose to believe her.

As time went on, it seemed as if I never had a father around. The times he was home I wanted his attention and his love. As I look back, Mom made all the decisions when he wasn't there, and when he was there, it was rules, rules, and rules. I just don't think he was a stable influence in my life.

Chapter 7: My Partner in Crime

Jeaneen and I met some friends who lived down the street from where I lived. We used to go there and play card games like Gin Rummy and Canasta. We had great times, until one night Jeaneen's father came looking for her and came over to where we were.

Jeaneen didn't want us to tell him about her being there. So we hid her in the cabinet where the potatoes were stored. Our friends told Jeaneen's father that she wasn't there, but deep down inside, we knew he thought we were lying. He finally left. Jeaneen came out of the potato cabinet and profusely thanked us for hiding her.

Jeaneen's father thought he was very powerful and was very abrupt with everyone. I didn't particularly believe that, except that one day when we were hanging out together her father called the police to see where Jeaneen was. Of course she was with us. Only this time, a terrible thing happened!

The police took Jeaneen and me down to the station. They didn't take anyone else. Where were our parents? We didn't do anything wrong, and the police shouldn't have kept us.

They put us in a cell for one week. It was the scariest time of my young life thus far. Jeaneen's father had done this to us for no good reason. My mother tried to do everything in her limited power to help, but nothing seemed to work. My outlook on life was pretty sour at the time. The one person at my side was always my Mom, continuously telling me everything would be better soon. To this day I still don't know why I was in jail.

During my stay, the sheriff's wife was nice to us. She gave us things to do to keep us busy. She brought us delicious homemade food. Our cell doors weren't locked and were left open most of the time, but we knew if we left we would be arrested and taken back in, so why bother to leave. This happened during the school semester, so we missed school.

Mom would come by and see us every day. I could only see Mom from the outside of a window in the door. That's when the doors were locked tight. No one could come and see Jeaneen except my Mom. Jeaneen's mother wasn't allowed to visit because she had to take care of the smaller children. Her husband had forbidden it. She was a nice, quiet woman who was under her husband's control.

It seemed like forever, but the authorities finally released us. The police told us not to hang around together anymore. Also, Jeaneen's father told my mom that under no circumstances were we to hang around together. Those words were easier said than done.

It was very difficult having to walk down the street on opposite sides without yelling out, "Hello, there." Not being able to talk to Jeaneen at school was equally difficult.

About a month later after my jail stay, I went to visit a friend of mine. She was older than me, and married. Her husband drove a city bus from Junction City, Kansas, to Wichita, Kansas, and back again. In the past, Jeaneen and I would ride the bus just to look at the scenery. It was such fun at the time. They were a nice, generous couple, and I was invited to stay for dinner on many occasions.

On this particular night, just before dinner, there was a knock at the door. Surprise, Jeaneen was at the door!

What a sight to see my friend and be able to actually talk with her. I couldn't remember the last time we could just chat. Our friends knew about Jeaneen's father so they were just trying to be nice and surprised me by inviting Jeaneen over.

During supper we heard a car pull up in front of the house and you wouldn't believe it; it was the police. They were looking for Jeaneen.

The police came to the door as Jeaneen ran out the back door, running, running as fast as her legs could carry her. Then the police saw me, asked me to go outside, and as I did they grabbed me and put handcuffs on me and took me off to jail, again.

They didn't allow me to explain. I asked why they were arresting me, and the police said it was because I was hanging out with Jeaneen. On the way, I could hear the police radio say they found Jeaneen and were bringing her in as well. I couldn't understand what was going on but I didn't have any choice in the matter.

Jeaneen had to stay for less than a week, but I was in jail for a month. I was very confused. I just had my Mom, and we didn't have a lot of money in those days. There wasn't much she could do. She couldn't retain a lawyer, and I am not sure if there were any pro-bono lawyers in those days.

She did speak to a lawyer, but he said nothing could be done. Basically, this was because Jeaneen's big shot father "owned" half the town. We were overruled and let down.

Mom and I wanted to tell Dad, but we didn't know where to write, or how to get in touch with him. He wrote very sporadically, and Mom didn't always know where to reach him. When the month of jail time was up, I went to court. I don't know to this day what the charges were.

We were in a teeny, tiny room. The judge was sitting behind his desk. Those present were Mom, myself, Jeaneen, her father, their lawyer, and someone from the court. There was a lot of talking and arguing between the other people. My mom stayed quiet because she didn't understand what was going on.

I listened closely and never heard so many lies in my life stated about Jeaneen and myself. I wasn't allowed to speak in my own behalf, I suppose because we didn't have a lawyer or maybe I was too young. In any case the judge didn't ask either Jeaneen or me any questions.

It didn't take very long for the judge to make a decision. All of a sudden, the judge grabbed his gavel, pounded it and declared, "This is enough! The two girls are to be sent to the industrial school until they're eighteen." Jeaneen's dad looked smug and didn't say anymore. My Mom broke down and sobbed, "No, no, no!"

Eveline Sandy

Chapter 8: Beloit

When the judge slammed down his gavel, all I could think of was, 'Eighteen; that is forever!'

I couldn't believe what I heard from the judge's lips since we didn't do anything wrong. Mom had tears pouring down her face; she was never without me for this length of time. Dad was gone, and now, I would be gone too.

That night I got to go home with Mom, and oh, how I wanted to just stay there and hide and never leave our home again.

The next day Mom was allowed to accompany me in the police cruiser to the industrial school. It took over three hours to get there, and I was horrified when we arrived, Finally, I had to say good-bye to Mom. I clung to her and reluctantly let her go when the house mother arrived to get me.

The Beloit Juvenile Correctional Facility was basically a home for wayward girls. It was founded with the idea to keep youthful offenders away from the influence of adult offenders. It just recently closed after one hundred years of being in existence.

If you did a Web search you would find two different mind sets about the facility. Basically, in the months I was incarcerated there, a person's infractions could be very, very simple in order to get sentenced to stay there. Some suggest the facility worked the girls constantly and were mean to them.

I was lucky, that with the housing I had, and with the housemother's and my Mom's support, it wasn't as difficult for me as some girls state. I never felt like a "bad" girl, but rather someone that was in the wrong place at the wrong time.

I was put in a cottage dorm with seven other girls. The grounds were not fenced in. We stayed put, because if we left without permission, we would get more time.

The girls were there for all different reasons. One was there for burning cats; and one didn't listen to her parents, so they dumped her at Beloit. There were charges from ridiculous to serious. I couldn't tell them what I did, because I didn't know.

I still don't know. Maybe it was the misfortune of having a friendship with Jeaneen and following what she did.

We had house mothers who lived with us all the time. There were four of them to cover the twenty-four-hour period during the week and the weekend. I enjoyed sitting with them and talking. I told them all about my Mom and Dad and how much we had been through in my lifetime. I didn't tell them about the rape, because I didn't want them to go back and tell Mom and Dad.

Beloit Juvenile Correctional Facility

How I always wanted to just have a happy normal life, living with Mom and Dad. There were times I would wonder what "normal" was really like. Dad was off in the war, and Mom was alone. She was much sadder than ever before. What a family we had now, as we were scattered all over.

We never gave up though. There were nights I would stay awake and just think how someday, I would be able to go home again. I lived for that day.

Truly, the house mothers were wonderful to me. I didn't give them any trouble, so they had no cause to get stern with me. There were times when they would tell me that if there was a way, I could possibly go home. They couldn't figure out why I was there in the first place.

In the beginning of my stay, I had trouble sleeping. I didn't trust the other girls, I missed my Mom, and felt exposed. I told my housemothers, and one told me to get my pillow and blanket and come lay down in the opening under her desk in her office. I would fall asleep, because I felt safe and secure.

Not all the housemothers would allow that privilege. On those nights I would cry myself to sleep. Sometimes, I would lean up against a window pane in my room and look up at the stars. Later I would write to Mom and tell her about the stars twinkling in the sky.

Time passed. I was placed in the facility in October, and I realized I was going to spend Thanksgiving, as well as Christmas there. I was worried I might not see Mom during the Holidays.

Mom did find someone to drive her out to visit me. I had a girlfriend, P.J., and she would visit a family member with her mom and dad and they would bring my Mom with them.

It was Christmas Eve, and we were sitting in the school's living room. Some of us got to go home for the Holiday on passes. I didn't get one. I was very miserable and homesick. All I could do was think about Mom.

All of Mom's family was in Germany and she hadn't seen them since I was seven. I was now thirteen years of age. My Dad's parents didn't acknowledge my Mom or me during this time, so we were alone. I fantasized my present to my Mom would be for her to see her family again. What a fabulous dream!

Mom kept in contact with our family in Germany. She had a lot of pride though; when they asked how things were, she would never tell them how bad it was with Dad, or how poor we had it. Maybe it wasn't pride; maybe she didn't want to worry them, because they didn't have a lot to share.

Mom continued to dream of returning to Germany for a visit. You never know; it could happen… You never give up on your dreams. It what keeps us all hoping and having faith for a better time.

Later that evening, there was a knock on the cottage door as I was watching television in the living room. The housemother answered the door, and she gave a gasp.

What a miracle, it was my Mom! Both of our faces were filled with joy! Mom wasn't supposed to come in, but the housemother said, "It's fine. Come on in and see Evie."

Mom couldn't stay very long because the people she rode in with were waiting patiently outside. We spent most of our time hugging and kissing each other. That was the best surprise present I ever got…my Mom!

Mom brought me an apple crate filled with little knick-knacks wrapped in newspaper. She still didn't have a lot of money and definitely had none for wrapping paper, so newspaper had to do.

She told me she wanted to buy me more, and I told her that no present could be bought with the love and joy she gave me by coming to visit me. It was more than enough.

It came time to say goodbye, and lots of tears flowed down our cheeks. Oh, how I wanted to go home. Still, it wouldn't be for quite some time. My heart was breaking, but I had to make the best of it.

Christmas Day was very lonely. Mom didn't have phone service in her home, so I couldn't wish her a Merry Christmas, or hear her sweet voice.

Don't get me wrong, it was okay at the cottage because I have a naturally friendly personality. A lot of the girls were jealous of me, because I had a mother who cared. Most of them had no one, or had parents that never visited.

At times I also felt abandoned, but deep down inside, I knew Mom was there for me, even if she couldn't travel to see me.

At that point, I felt older than my thirteen years. I went to school, had nice teachers and had chores to do. I had kitchen duty three times a day. They sure kept us busy at all times. At night we would sit around and watch a small television, or listen to music.

Each of us had to take turns making snacks at night. On the weekends, we had to clean our dorms and wash and wax the floors.

It was funny when I had to clean the dorm by myself, especially using the buffer after waxing the floor. The big machine would take me all over the floor. It was so heavy, and I was so tiny. I was only 100 pounds. I think I was assigned to do the buffing all the time because it was so funny seeing me get dragged around.

Jeaneen was sent to the same reformatory school as me for the same amount of time. She was placed in a different cottage, and we hardly ever saw each other. We did say hello to each other when we could, which wasn't very often.

She didn't like it there at all and tried to run away several times, so they put her in security lockup for awhile. I didn't understand why she kept trying to run away. All she had to do was put up with what they wanted all of us to do: keep the rules, go to school, do the chores. What's the big deal?

Sure, there were times I wanted to leave, but I also realized that someday I would go home if I could endure this situation. I saw a lot of the other girls eventually go home.

We were given privileges when the housemother's felt they could trust us. We went to the movies on weekends, or roller skating. They had a work furlough for the older girls.

The facility housed girls from ages ten to eighteen. Some of the girls had to work to make extra money for themselves, because it wasn't a free ride. The girls that were allowed to work could be trusted. Some of the girls had financial backing from their parents and didn't have to work. They seemed to be snobby and didn't associate with us peons that didn't have money.

On Sundays we were required to attend church services. I would see Jeaneen in church, and we would say hello. She was so sorry for what her father did to us. I told her it wasn't her fault. She was filled with such hatred for him.

I blended with the other girls as best as I could. I even got my ears pierced there. Of course the housemothers didn't know that, or else they looked the other way.

Time went on, and it was just before Easter when there was a phone call for me. I thought it was my Mom calling for me, but surprise, it was my father!

He said the reason why Mom and I hadn't heard from him before was because he was wounded in the war. Dad was calling from a military hospital in California. He told me he would have written but he couldn't because both his hands were hurt very badly, and he couldn't hold a pen. I am not sure if that was the truth or not. When I saw him he didn't have any scars on his hands. So what do I believe?

Dad told me over and over, he loved me very much, and as soon as he got better, he would see if I could come home sooner. First he would come and visit me. We said our tearful good-byes and hung up.

Dad sent me some money for stamps and extra things like material to make clothes in home economics class. There was a little extra money for soda pop and candy as well. Boy, did I feel special. We had our lockers upstairs, and if we had soda pop, or anything of value we would place it in there. The housemothers were the only ones with the keys to open the lockers.

Easter weekend came, and Dad was coming to see me. I was really excited. The housemother called my name and I went into Mr. Crown's office, and there was my Dad! What a sight to actually see Dad after almost three years. We left for a full day's pass and it was wonderful!

One of the classes I took at Beloit was sewing. I soon learned to design and sew all my clothes. I became very adept at it, and it was a long time before I had store-bought clothes. Dad took me shopping and bought me some new clothes: dresses, shoes and underwear.

He bought me one hot pink and one green dress. They were very gaudy. They were very proper though, with high necklines and knee length skirts. Those dresses would be important to me in the future.

Our day off campus was so much fun. We stopped off to have a soda, and I told Dad about my friends at the cottage and how they didn't get much attention from their families. So we stopped at another store, and Dad bought all the girls in my cottage Easter baskets and sodas.

The girls were all surprised at that and were chattering and thanking my Dad. Dad and I had a super visit, and before he left he had a long, serious talk with me. He told me he was deeply sorry for the way he treated Mom and none of it was my fault. I felt better when he told me this, but I really wanted him to tell me we were going to be a family again.

Dad said he had something very important to tell me. He showed me a photo of a Korean woman with a little girl and said that he met her overseas. Dad told me that the little girl was his, and she was my sister. Her name was Mylynn. He said that if he and Mom did not stay together, he wanted me to come and live with him..

I felt terribly sad and confused. I bravely told Dad that I could never leave Mom because I loved her so much. I loved my Dad very much as well, but the fact was Mom was always there for me, and Dad wasn't always in the picture.

I feel my dad always tried to sabotage my relationship with my mother. He acknowledged that I was the most important person in my Mom's life and vice-versa. Yet he continuously told me bad things he did and then said, "Evie, don't tell your mom."

Today, I realize he was not a good role model for me. It was a terrible burden for a small child to carry. Did he set me up and know I would go tell my mom so he wouldn't have to? Didn't he have the guts and honesty to talk with my Mom himself? I just didn't get it.

He didn't once say, "I love you, Evie." He didn't explain why he did this terrible thing to my Mom with another woman. He didn't say he would stay with Mom and me and give up the Korean woman and his daughter, Mylynn. He didn't say where he had been. He appeared to lack emotion. I didn't feel loved by him. I felt empty and abandoned. I felt I wasn't worthy of his love.

"What did I do wrong?" Once again, this thought troubled me.

Dad left it at that and didn't say anymore on the subject. On the way back to the cottage, we stopped, and Dad bought me some goodies to keep in my locker. That day went by so fast, probably because I was having such a great time with Dad up until he showed me the photo.

He told me that it wouldn't be long before I would be coming home again for good. He said it might be another month; no more.

I don't know how he knew that. At that point I wasn't sure I really wanted to go home. What would happen? Would Dad be gone for good? When would he say to Mom what he said to me?

Dad said to start packing my things and getting prepared to come home soon. About two weeks later I got a pass to go home for a week. I couldn't wait to see Mom again; it had been awhile since she had been here.

Apparently, Dad went home to Mom. They came together to pick me up, and we all went back to Junction City, Kansas. We went to see Aunt Hazel and her two boys again.

It was a great but very strange feeling. I had to readjust and feel part of life again. No one would understand that unless they had been through the same circumstances that I had been in just how difficult it is to "fit into" society. I felt like everyone was staring at me.

Mom and Dad appeared to be happy together again. I didn't say anything about that Korean woman and her daughter and who the father was. I figured we would continue to live together as a family. I didn't want to be blamed for breaking up the family, because I didn't do anything wrong.

The first week went by extremely fast, and it was time to return to the cottage. I felt very sad inside. I knew it wouldn't be much longer until I was home for good, because my Dad said so. I told my roommates at the cottage about it, and they said it was almost impossible to go home for good. They told me not to get my hopes up.

About a week later, Mr. Crown called me into his office and said he had a long talk with both my Dad and Mom. Mr. Crown decided that since both parents were home to raise me, I could go home permanently.

We would be leaving the state of Kansas as well, because Dad got new orders. It was May of 1967. I was fourteen-years-old.

Dad came up with some fairy-tale story to get me out of there. I was thankful, but doubtful of the truth of any of Dad's story to Mr. Crown. However he did it, I was grateful. Wow, I never thought I would really hear those wonderful words, "You're going home for good."

I walked out of his office with the biggest, fattest grin on my face. I said a silent prayer of thanks to God. I told all the housemothers I was leaving in another week for good, and they congratulated me. They had already known the great news but had to wait until Mr. Crown told me first.

Most of the girls were happy for me, telling me they wished it was them going home. Those that weren't happy were the ones that didn't have a mother or father to go home to. I felt sorry for them.

I told them when they finally got released, not to make the same mistakes, and get a good job so they could be proud of themselves. I also told them not to give up and to keep hoping for the best. Somehow, someday, things would improve, even at the worst moments in life.

I started thinking about Jeaneen and what would happen to her. Her father wasn't about to allow her to go home. He told her she was staying until she was eighteen and that was final!

Her mother didn't have much say in the matter, and I suppose her father never allowed her to visit Jeaneen either. I felt very sad for Jeaneen. Her father also said he didn't want to have anything to do with her ever again. I don't know if her mom was included in all that. I felt so bad for her.

The last thing I heard about her was she got a town job. Knowing I probably will never see her again, I continue to pray for my best friend. I hope she is doing well in life.

It was time to leave, and some of the girls gave me their addresses and took mine and asked me to write to them. They wanted to know any updates on how I was getting along in life. That was sure nice of them!

After I returned home, I did want to write to a few of the girls but my father said "No." He ordered me with, "You are starting over and need to leave the past alone." I was sad I couldn't contact any of my roomies, and sometimes I was tempted to write, but I never did.

All the housemothers said goodbye and wished me luck. They said I was very fortunate to get out early, and I would do just fine. They were positive about this.

There's an old saying that says: "When you leave down that long road away from there, don't look back."

Eveline Sandy

Chapter 9: Off To Grandparent's House We Go

When we left the town where the facility was located, Dad put Mom and I on a bus to my grandparents' home. The reason was, he had to get everything ready where we were going to live. That was okay by me; I wanted to see my grandparents again. They couldn't visit me at the industrial school because they lived so far away. The bus ride wasn't very long, and Grandpa picked us up and took us to his home.

At first, they treated me a little differently, knowing where I had been. Within a few days the ice broke, and everyone acted like nothing had happened. They were very good to me. I got to go and visit all my friends. I didn't have to go to summer school because I had passed to ninth grade at the facility. I had a fabulous summer there.

Finally, one day, Dad called and said all of our things were going to be picked up and we were going to move to Fort Lewis, Washington. I said goodbye to Grandpa and Grandma and the rest of the family and we were off again. It seemed just like old times, moving around so much. Ugh.

We arrived in Washington, and stayed on base in a room until Dad found us an apartment; even though he said he was going to have everything ready for us. It was a cute little one bedroom apartment; as Dad couldn't afford more.

The next day while Dad was at work there was a knock at the door. Mom opened it, and it was Knut. He was someone we knew when we lived in Germany and had lost touch with. Apparently, somewhere on the base, Mom had run into Knut's parents and told them where we lived. Knut stopped over to pay his respects. He was a bit older than me and kind of cute. Knut wanted to know if he could take me to the show. Mom answered immediately, "No way," because my father was real strict when it came to me going anywhere.

I know Knut was trying to be nice, but I am glad Mom said no. I was still pretty fearful of boys because of what had happened to me when I was twelve.

When we finally moved from base housing to the apartment, a coincidence happened. The Anderson's lived in a house right across the street from where we were. Mom and I would go over and visit Knut's mom and reminisce on times in Germany. She would show us photos from when both Knut and I were children. It was neat to look at them.

We could only do this visiting when Dad wasn't home. He didn't want Mom to have friends. I don't know why. I just felt it was strange and kind of like sneaking around even though I knew it wasn't wrong.

It was school time again and I attended Lakes High School. I met some great people and made some really nice friends. I went swimming on the weekends right in the neighborhood. It was a pond of sorts. Washington weather is wet; talk about liquid sunshine. I believe Washington has the greatest rainfall in the United States.

Anyway, it seemed as soon as we would get to the swimming pond, it would start raining. We would get out of the pond, get our belongings together and then it would stop raining. It was so exasperating!

Chapter 10: Mom, My Pillar

After we got settled, my mom became friends with our neighbor, Germaine Maine.

Mom and Mrs. Maine liked each other a lot even though she was much younger than Mom. Mrs. Maine didn't speak German, but they both had a lot to share. We all became really close. We would go to each other's homes to eat together and had fun time as well. I still stay in touch with her to this day. She is an angel!

During our stay there, around 1968, my Mom became ill. She started spotting blood in between her periods. I suggested she go see a doctor, but she just ignored my pleas and said she would be fine. No one ever said anything to Dad that I know of.

I did go over to Germaine's and told her about it. I knew she wouldn't tell Mom I had told her. The next day, Germaine came over and began talking with Mom and "found" out Mom was ill. Mom then decided, at Germaine's urging, to go to a doctor on base.

What a relief. Sometimes I was just weary of being the adult. Mom made an appointment in a few days, and Maine went with her while I was in school. I didn't have much of a good day because I was worried about what the doctor would say about Mom. When I came home, Mom didn't look happy at all.

She sat me down at the kitchen table and said she had some bad news to tell me. I couldn't imagine what it was. I thought I was in trouble. I wish I was. Mom told me the doctors told her that she had uterine cancer and had to have surgery within a week.

My heart felt as if it went to my feet and didn't want to work. I cried and cried and couldn't stop; this was my mom. Cancer! The Big C! I couldn't lose her. At first, I thought the worst; that she would die, and what would I do without my mother?

Mom went to the hospital and had the initial surgery. She had a hysterectomy, and it was pretty bad in those days. The doctors found the cancer had spread and had to cut more parts out of her. Some of her nerves were severed. Consequently, the recuperation time lasted for weeks and weeks.

She was in the Fort Lewis Hospital for three months. She had to learn to walk again and was extremely weak. I don't know all the details, but I am sure she had chemotherapy. That has always been a pretty standard practice for cancer.

I did go to school every day, because that's what Mom wanted. I didn't like Mom being away so long, but knew that's how it had to be. We were always getting separated, but our hearts were like one. Germaine, the angel lady, would help me out when she could.

It was just Dad and I living at the apartment, essentially. I think Dad really took this illness with Mom very badly. He started drinking a lot.

One night I was at home in bed and Dad came in and put his arm around me. He smelled bad because he had been drinking. I felt my "red flags" coming up and it could have been since my rape I didn't feel comfortable with any man's touch, even with my Dad's hugs.

I don't know if he touched me inappropriately, or just reached out to comfort me because Mom was gone. I just remember I got really scared and slapped him hard and told him to get out of my room.

We never discussed that night, and we never had the chance later on, because he moved out the next day and went to live on the base barracks. I wish sometimes that we could talk it out. I know I have forgiven him; I just can't forget it. It was one of those tough times I had to live through.

I lived in the apartment by myself for three months. Dad would bring me money for food, pay all the bills and give me money for school. He wouldn't stop by when I was home, but rather would leave the money on the kitchen table when I was at school. We were all going through changes.

One day, Maine came over and said she would take me to see Mom. The staff refused us and said I was too young. Maine told me to wait in the hallway until she saw Mom. Well, I waited until the staff was all down at the other end of the hall, and I snuck into Mom's room. Maine was a sweetheart for doing that.

I took one look at Mom and sucked in my breath. My mother was lying in the bed so white she looked dead to me. I ran back out into the hallway and fainted. One of the nurses saw me laying there and gave me a shot of some kind of medicine to bring me around. Whatever it was helped me to calm down about who I just saw: my beloved Mom. The nurse told me Mom would be alright, and to just give her some time.

Now, I understand why the staff didn't want me to go in and see Mom in her condition. The effects of the chemotherapy were evident on her face and body. She had quite a battle with cancer.

I went back into the room, and Mom woke up to see me standing next to her bed. She tried to talk but was too weak to speak clearly. I stayed for a little bit and then kissed her and said, "I will be back, Momma. I love you, Momma." Later that same evening Dad went and tried to be nice to Mom. I am not sure if he succeeded.

I went back to visit Mom a few days later, since the doctors agreed now to let me go and see her. Mom was now in intense therapy to learn how to walk again. It was difficult for her, but she also had that German resilience with a strong will to live.

At one point the doctors spoke to Dad and me, and said Mom was going to need cobalt-radiation. They didn't have the proper machinery to administer it at the Fort Lewis hospital in those days. They said she would have to go to the Walter Reed Medical Center in Washington, D.C. for her treatments.

Dad made the arrangements and had Mom moved. I felt like I had to grow up fast. I told Mom I loved her and we would see each other before too long. That was the most difficult day I lived through. I didn't know if I would see her again. I didn't know if Dad would be there for me. I didn't know where I was going to live. I didn't know what the future would bring. I was scared. There were no answers.

Eveline Sandy

Chapter 11: He's Not Coming Back

Well, I still lived in the apartment by myself until one day Dad came over for once during the time I was home and had news. He said we were moving to D.C. right away where Mom was because his retirement was up. He had spent twenty-three years in the Army. What a long haul.

Out of those twenty-three years I was with him for almost fifteen years, and we sure moved around a lot. So here we go again. At least this time, the move would take us back to Mom.

Maine wrote a letter to my school explaining the move was due to an illness in the family and got my records for me. I cleaned the whole apartment by myself so we could get the deposit back. I packed everything up.

Dad showed up early, packed everything in the truck and said, "Let's go." He explained he would put me on a plane by myself and I was going stay at my aunt's until he drove all our belongings there, and then he would pick me up and we would go to Mom in D.C. It sounded like a plan.

I went to say goodbye to Maine and thank her for all help. (Isn't it funny how many good- byes I have had to say in my lifetime?) I didn't have time to change my clothes after cleaning the apartment because Dad was in such a hurry.

When we got to the airport, I told Dad I had to change my clothes before I boarded the plane. Dad said okay and handed me $800.00 in cash, my ticket, and said, "I will see you later." He also said, "I love you very much."

I went into the bathroom, changed and came back out; then I looked around and said "Where is Dad?"

He was gone! I had the funniest, sinking feeling in the pit of my stomach that I had never experienced before. At first I didn't want to get on the plane because I felt I would never see Dad again. Nevertheless, I turned around and walked towards the gate where my flight was leaving. I got on the plane after a few moments of indecision and all I was thinking was 'Why did Dad leave so suddenly?" At the same time I was also hoping Mom was doing better.

That was the last time I saw my dad. It was April, 1968.

I had never flown by myself before. The plane stopped off in Chicago for a four hour lay-over, and I was scared. I was all alone in such a huge airport at the age of fifteen. I decided to call my aunt and let her know about the layover and the possibility of being late. I really didn't know who was picking me up at the airport when I arrived.

When my Aunt Laura answered the phone, she was happy to hear from me, but didn't have any idea that I was coming to stay with her. I realized then that something was definitely wrong.

I didn't know what to do at that point. At first she didn't want me to come to her. After a few moments of my pleading with her, telling her my dad would be there in a week to pick me up she said, "It's okay honey, come on to Delta and we will pick you up."

So off I went to Delta, Ohio to start the next episode of my life. I had to change planes, and when it finally arrived in Delta, the airport was closed. I had to wait outside until my aunt arrived. Finally, she arrived and retrieved my one suitcase and got me in the car. I was really tired and confused. Once again, the feeling of abandonment set in me. I didn't like it at all. I just felt like what else could possibly happen to me, and whatever it was, I probably wouldn't be surprised.

At first everything was alright at Aunt Laura's. I helped her do the dishes and cooked and cleaned. It was the way my mom taught me.

About a week later, I hadn't heard from Dad; he never called, or showed up. Aunt Laura asked me if I had any money and I said "Yes, I do." She asked how much.

I made a big mistake by telling her how much Dad gave me. She said it was too much for me to have, and she needed it to take care of me. So I gave the $800.00 to her and never saw it again.

My Aunt Laura wasn't a witch. I believe she was just tired of how her brother treated her. I think she took out her frustrations on me because of it. I did have compassion for her because she was a loving, kind person.

Aunt Laura enrolled me in high school in the fall of 1968. I started ninth grade in Delta. I had a new home, a new school, and new friends. I was going to adjust to my new surroundings again.

I spoke to Mom and she didn't realize I was with Aunt Laura. Dad hadn't talked with her since she left for Washington. Dad gave Mom the same story about all of us living together in Washington.

I told Mom everything would be okay. I didn't want to tell her all the details about the airport and Aunt Laura not knowing I was coming to live with her. I didn't want to worry her under the circumstances. I told her Dad would come here before too long. The conversation was short because she wasn't feeling very well.

Shortly after that I got a call from my grandparents. Aunt Laura had let them know I was staying with her. My dad didn't let anyone know thus far, about plans for myself and Mom. I found out from my grandparents that Dad had taken a plane back overseas and was going to live there permanently. No good byes, no messages, no nothing. Now I really didn't know what was going to happen. My family was divided and no adults were making decisions. I felt the weight of the world on my thin shoulders.

I wasn't worried about myself as much as I was worried about Mom. When would she get better? When would she be let out of the rehab center? Where would she go when she was released? There wasn't any home anymore.

I don't think anyone heard from Dad. In my thoughts, he totally abandoned us. He left my mom to heal by herself from a horrible disease and left me, his adopted daughter, with an unknown future. How could he be so cruel to us?

***

One day all my friends were going to the roller rink. I asked my aunt for permission to go and she said, "Well, you can go for two hours, and no more." So off we went.

When we arrived I noticed some guy there in a leather jacket. He kept coming over to talk to me. He asked me if he could see me later, and I told him loudly, "Leave me alone! I'm not allowed to date." He continued to follow me around. I was really bugged and those "red flags" were up high and flying in the breeze. Finally it was time to leave, and I went back home to Aunt Laura's.

About a week later there was a knock at the door and it was him! (I didn't know his name, and I didn't want to.) He asked to talk to me and my aunt blew her stack. She was very protective of me since my stay at the Beloit Juvenile Facility and laid down the rules when I came to live with her. Rule number one was: No Boys!

She told that boy to leave and never come back. She didn't say a word to me. I went to sleep that night on the couch, wondering what she was going to say to me about the subject.

I was scared. What if she told me I couldn't live there anymore? I had no one else to turn to. Was my life supposed to be mostly made up of pain and anger? I didn't know. I am not sure I even cared at that moment.

I later found out, that the boy asked one of my friends who I was and where I lived, and my friend innocently told him. My aunt would never listen to my explanation. I tried and tried to tell her. I felt like a bad person.

The next morning, my uncle Donald, (Laura's husband) got up early and found me on the couch. He started making passes at me. I told him to back off and leave me alone. He said if I told my aunt, I would be in a lot of trouble! I ran to my room and shut and locked the door. I stayed in there until he went to work, and I heard Aunt Laura get up. I went to her and told her what happened with Uncle Donald. She wouldn't believe me.

What is it with adults not believing children? Don't you realize you adults are in power? When a child comes to you with pain and hurt in their eyes and tells you something horrible has happened to them, believe them. Be diligent in your efforts to prove or disprove what the child has stated.

But, initially, all you should do is remove the child from the danger and put them in a safe haven, no matter how temporary. Then take the steps of proper notification to the appropriate authority.

Kids don't always make things up, especially when it comes down to sexual assault or rape. Don't be in denial, it happens every day in the "real" world and it could happen to your own. Frankly, it will save that child from an everlasting world of hurt and bad effects of a lifetime. Some never recover to be mentally healthy, because of what has occurred in childhood.

My aunt completely ignored anything more I had to say about my Uncle Donald. After that, she never trusted anything I said. She said I was to be punished for that boy following me home and coming to the door.

I told her what happened at the rink, but she chose not to believe me. She told me that I had to stay in my room indefinitely and to come out only to go to the bathroom, eat at the table and attend school. I was so angry with her; I didn't want to have anything to do with her anymore, ever.

Approximately forty-three years later, after my Uncle Donald passed away, my aunt called me and asked if I had been telling her the truth about what he had done to me. I responded "Yes," and that I forgave my uncle long ago. I was at peace within, and she should do the same.

Soon after, one day while I was at school, I was called in to talk to someone in the counseling department. They asked me all kinds of questions, and I told them what happened to my mom and about my dad leaving me. I told them I didn't want to stay with my Aunt Laura anymore. I wanted to be with my mother. I didn't mention anything about Uncle Donald. I wanted to, but I didn't think anyone would believe me. I just wanted my Mom.

The counselor made a phone call to my aunt and had me talk with a representative from the American Red Cross. They called my mom in Washington, D.C., and she explained that the reason I was there with Aunt Laura was because she was in the hospital getting cancer treatments, and her husband was gone.

Afterwards, the American Red Cross rep spoke to me some more and agreed I needed to go to my mother and they would pay for my flight and the taxi service.

I went back to Aunt Laura's and packed my belongings in my suitcase and took it to the school that night as the American Red Cross representative instructed me. I never said anything, not even a good bye to my aunt.

When I went to school as usual the next morning, the American Red Cross was waiting for me and took me directly to the airport.

I felt much better inside, not like when I flew to Delta to live with my aunt. It wouldn't be long and I would be able to see my mother again. I was one happy camper!

When the taxi pulled up in front of the hospital rehab building, there, at the top of the stairs, stood my Mom, in the beautiful green dress that my dad had bought for me at Beloit. I remember the scene to this day.

Chapter 12: A Sight For Sore Eyes.

I ran as fast as I could up the stairs of the hospital. The aroma of the cherry blossoms filled me up. I reached the top and grabbed my Mom hugging and kissing her. It had been so long since I saw her so healthy. That was the best thing that happened to me; to be reunited with my mother! I was hoping it was for good this time.

Mom did look a little different than before. The radiation had really taken a toll on her. She was smaller and older looking.

When we got into the hospital, the staff had arranged for me to stay in her room with her. They had placed a bed in her room for me. I ate the hospital food along with Mom.

I met a lot of servicemen that got hurt during the Viet Nam War. They all seemed nice and enjoyed having someone from the outside to talk with. I played checkers with some of them, and I learned all the moves. Some of them were going home soon to their families, and others were going to be in rehab for a long time. It was kind of sad.

When they talked about "'Nam" they told me it was the worst experience they had in their entire lives. When I spoke with the soldiers, I could then understand some of the changes I saw Dad go through.

I told them about Mom's cancer and about Dad abandoning us, because I guess Dad couldn't handle being in the war and coping with Mom's illness so soon afterwards.

We never heard from Dad and consequently didn't have any more money from him either. Mom and I were destitute until the American Red Cross came to the rescue again and gave us some money to live on.

Soon, the hospital staff told Mom that I couldn't stay at the hospital with her anymore. So Mom and I went looking for a room for us to stay in for a short time. We did find one not far from the hospital, so we could walk back and forth. Mom still had more treatments to complete.

Not long after, I became very ill, so Mom had to go back to the hospital in the snow and get medicine for me and bring food back. There was no place to cook food in the room. It was simply a room to sleep in. It was difficult on Mom because along with getting the daily treatments, she was weak and tired most of the time.

After I got better, the doctors told Mom that we could move to the annex, which was part of the hospital. It didn't cost us anything, but the down side was, we would have to take the bus back and forth to where Mom received her treatments.

It was okay but not really a home. The main thing was I got to stay in Mom's room with her once again. The nursing staff was very kind and helpful. There were a lot of servicemen there also.

It was getting close to the Holidays and Mom and I had nothing to give to each other for gifts. I know our true gift to each other was being together again. I always prayed for Mom each night, that she would be cancer-free and healthy. It would take a miracle, I knew, but both of us possessed a tremendous amount of faith and we would never give up.

We all go through hard times, some more than others, and I believe from the bottom of my heart, that there is another day and another chance for happiness. Just hang in there and enjoy the time that you are able to be here on this earth. A doorway of opportunity is just around the corner. Never give up hope.

A lot of people take their lives for granted and don't enjoy the moment. Whether it is full of strife, or challenge we learn from our experiences and our characters develop. If we had a soft life, it would be very boring, right? If the happy times are few and far between, take time to smell the roses. Mom and I certainly learned that the hard way. I lost my Mom early on in life and I wish every minute of my day I could have her back in my life for a moment. Each day we experience is precious and cannot be repeated, and we have no idea what will happen next.

Chapter 13: A Miracle Happens

    One day Mom was taking a nap, so I decided to go for a walk. Thinking we needed a real home for both of us, I prayed and knew we would get one soon. As I prayed, I walked around the neighborhood. There was one street that was steep to walk, but I did anyway. About halfway through the street, there was this huge house with a sign out front with, "Apartment for Rent".
    I decided to go in and talk with the folks. So, I knocked at the door and an elderly gentleman opened the door and said, "Yes, may I help you young lady?"
    I replied, "Yes, I am looking for a home for my mother and me."
    He looked at me funny, probably wondering what a young girl was doing looking for a home. I explained about Mom and me, and what happened to us in the last few months. The gentleman told me his name was Mr. O'Brian and the apartment was $100.00 a month with utilities included. I boldly told Mr. O'Brian I was going to look for a job and when I found one I would be back. Would he please hold the apartment for us?
    Mr. O'Brian looked down at me and smiled and said, "My child, you and your mother can move in right away and live in the apartment for three months free! All you have to do is help me clean my house." I was so excited and happy. I gushed, "Thank you, we will take it, and God bless you Mr. O'Brian!"
    My heart was racing 100 miles an hour. I ran down the block, anxious to get back to Mom and tell her the fantastic news. There are many goodhearted people in the world; probably more than evil ones. I have encountered many sweet, generous and loving people in my lifetime.
    I ran all the way up the hill inside the annex, to my Mom's room. I woke Mom up and said, "I have terrific news, Mom! We have a home to live in together."
    Mom said, "Calm down Evie, and tell me what you are talking about?" So I told her about the apartment and also told her we didn't need linens, or dishes, or any household items. The apartment was fully furnished and even had a washer and dryer!

When Dad and I left the apartment in Tacoma, Washington, he took all our household belongings that equipped a home. Basically, Mom and I really had nothing. We had the clothes on our backs and nothing more.

I have major issues with my dad. He brought us here from Germany to abandon us years later, broke and homeless. He wasn't a very good Dad or husband in my estimation.

Later, my grandparents told us that Dad had left some things with them for us to use whenever we could come and pick them up. There wasn't any furniture; I don't know what Dad did with that.

We didn't have money to live on, much less travel to pick up our belongings. I guess it didn't occur to my grandparents to ship them to us. So it was a blessing when I found the furnished apartment from Mr. O'Brian.

My mom was skeptical, but I told her we didn't have to pay rent for three months, and we could move in right away. Mom looked lovingly at me and said, "*Was ich wurde, ohmne meinen kleinen Engel auskommen?*" "What would I do without my little Angel?"

We both spoke to the doctors and they gave permission for her to move. Within a few days we packed, and we intended to walk to our new home in Mr. O'Brian's house. To my surprise, Mr. O'Brian insisted on giving me taxi fare so I could bring my weak mother in style to her new home. As I said we didn't have much, just our clothes, with a suitcase for each of us. We got settled in and Mom looked so happy for a change. The worried look slowly disappeared.

I told Mom that even though we could live there for free for three months, with me just cleaning Mr. O'Brian's home, I still wanted to find a job.

Mr. O'Brian was a sweetie. He was sickly, but had a heart of gold. He didn't live with his wife and truly needed care-giving. He was retired and never asked for anything. His children lived nearby and treated him respectfully, as they did my mother. I was happy to clean for him.

I still had to enroll in high school as well. This time it was Montgomery Blair High. I had to catch a bus to get there, because it was on the other side of town. Ugh.

When I started school I was introduced to Mr. Farley, my high school counselor. I told him about my current home life and said I needed to work as soon as I could to help out with the bills. I was only in ninth grade at the time, and Mr. Farley told me ninth graders couldn't work until they were in the tenth grade.

He decided to make an exception to help me out. Mr. Farley met with my mother, and Mom said in her broken English, "I have a very special daughter. Not many would do what she is willing to do."

After they chatted some more Mr. Farley wished my Mom well and left. The next day, when I went to school, I received great news. Mr. Farley found a job for me in a bakery at the Hecht Company, in Silver Springs, Maryland.

It was far from where we lived. I would get up early and go to school, get out early and then go to work. I took the city bus. From the bus to my home, I had to still walk over the bridge, which went over the freeway. In total, I walked about six blocks.

At times I was scared walking in the dark, and the bus driver noticed this. After he got to know me a bit, he would park his bus at the stop and told the passengers he would be right back. He would walk me across the bridge to the other side. He did that on a regular basis. What a kind person he was. I told you there were a lot of good people out there. I was so thankful to him.

I would bring Mom home a lot of goodies from the bakery. It's hard to explain, but Mother was so very proud of me. I told her when we needed each other there always is a way to get by.

At Christmas, Mr. O'Brian gave us a small tree. It was actually real and smelled heavenly. We always had "fake" trees. Out of the kindness of Mr. O'Brien's heart, we had a wonderful Christmas. We made homemade ornaments and other decorations for it.

There was one small present under the tree with my name on it from Mom. I was totally surprised. I opened it and there were a pair of silver silk stockings with a garter belt. (In those days nylon pantyhose weren't designed as yet, so only stockings were available.) Oh how my mom knew what I wanted! That one small gift meant more to me than a lot of others things I ever received in my life. I thanked her so much. I knew how difficult it was for Mom to get them for me.

I do hope you learn something from this, especially the readers that have been fortunate enough to have a good life with things that come easily to them. It's truly the thought that counts and not the size or cost of the gift!

Mom and I had our ups and downs; it seemed sometimes like a continual nightmare especially when Dad abandoned us. When you go through your difficulties did you all have the love, trust and faith that it took to get by ? Did you pray for guidance?

It does take patience for someone who doesn't really understand what's happening in their lives. I am not saying I have or haven't had a lot of the above. It's been a real struggle, trying to think positively. But I refused to give up, and neither should you. There's always another way.

At times I prevailed, and then at other times I used to think, "Stop the world I want to get off." I didn't want to know what would happen next.

We still hadn't heard from Dad. It was the same old lament. Mom would never talk badly about Dad, no matter what he did to us. Deep down inside she still loved him. Other women would probably have given up by now, but not Mom.

At times her inner strength was solid; she was someone I could always lean on. At other times, for a few moments, she would allow her true feelings to come out and she would cry.

When I brought my first paycheck home, it felt so good. I showed Mom and said, "I can buy you something nice now, Mutter." I went out and bought us some clothes. It had been so long since we had anything new.

It was a satisfying feeling, after working hard and then getting rewarded with the ability to buy something for Mom and myself.

It amazes me to this day how close Mom and I were, especially as a Mom and daughter. We thought alike. I could feel Mom's misgivings about her illness.

I prayed fervently that she could enjoy life for some time to come. Of course I couldn't predict how long she had. Any bit of time on earth would be better than losing her forever. I cherish every moment I had with her.

There's no one in this great big world who can tell you for sure what is going to happen next. You just do the best you can while you are here on earth. A lot of folks have to learn the words "a will to live." It is most important that you maintain a positive attitude.

You folks with a chronic, serious illness, might be around a lot longer if you maintain a positive attitude. Don't be in denial. Do what you have to do and deal with it in the best way while you have the time. Smell the roses, and enjoy life to the fullest. Live like you are here for only one more day on Earth. So let's get on with it.

Eveline Sandy

Chapter 14: My World Crashes Around Me

During the months just before Mr. O'Brien gave us the wonderful, real Christmas tree, a major event rocked my world.

Mom was gone for the day with a friend. I walked into the kitchen and saw a folder of papers laying there that I never saw before. I was very curious and opened the folder to find a top sheet that stated:

ORDER OF ADOPTION.
Year 1955
EVELINE DARLENE GABRIELA BEHM

I was in shock! I flipped through the rest of the papers and sat down heavily on the kitchen chair. Michael's name was on the second paper stating he was the adopting father. All my life I thought Michael was my blood father. For sixteen years my whole life revolved around the premise that he was my real and only father. Now I was looking down at papers that were telling me something totally different.

I started feeling faint and sick to my stomach. Thoughts were churning through my head, hammering me with questions:

What are these papers?
What does this mean?
Why isn't my dad my dad?
Should I confront my mom?
Who is my "real" dad?
Am I an illegitimate child?
Where do I go from here?
Why didn't my parents tell me?
Who else knows the truth?
Does everyone else know but me?
Why wasn't Mom honest with me?
Where is my real dad?
Why did he reject me?
"What did I do wrong?"

I was dumbfounded. Tears were pouring down my cheeks, and I was sobbing. I suddenly became angry and slammed the folder down on the table. I wanted to confront my mother. I had feelings of betrayal. I felt full of shame.

I ran out of the house and kept running and crying. It was midmorning on a Saturday. I didn't notice it was a beautiful day as I ran to the nearby park to escape.

I found an empty bench and sat down. I wanted no one around me. I didn't want anyone to talk with. I didn't have any family to talk to anyway. I felt my friends wouldn't understand my bewilderment. I needed to muddle through this on my own.

I turned to God, and begged Him to comfort me. I could confide in my Heavenly Father my sorrow and my pain. He never rejected me. He, above all, never turned His back on me. I felt His presence around me as he spoke within me. Slowly I started feeling at peace.

I spent the day huddled up in the corner of the bench, thinking and praying. Nightfall came. I wasn't hungry, I wasn't sad, I wasn't anything. I was totally numb from the experience. I finally fell asleep from mental exhaustion.

I awoke early on Sunday morning feeling refreshed, and even a bit hungry. I decided to go home and not say anything to Mom. I figured Mom would be gone for the whole weekend, so I wouldn't have to talk to her yet. But she was there and I greeted her as normal. She didn't ask me where I had been. She probably assumed I went out earlier in the morning. And life went on...

I kept wondering, "Why did Mom leave the "secret" papers on the table?" Well, our home was very small and storage wasn't abundant. I don't believe that the papers were purposely left there for me to look at. I believe it was a total accident that I looked at that horrible file.

I couldn't bring myself to further hurt her by a confrontation. It might have been different if my dad was still around then; I might have discussed the adoption with them. But he had abandoned me earlier at the airport.

This was not a closed issue with me. I always felt that someday in the future, my adopted father and I would reunite. I would ask him why Mom and he chose not to tell me the truth about my origins. I have, to this day, the adoption papers and original birth certificate. If I don't get the answers to the questions I have, it will be okay.

My belief is that parents should be honest with their children from the get-go. According to the child's age, give them limited information that they can handle. As they get older, give them detailed answers to their questions.. Reassure your children that they are loved. Always present life altering events in a very positive light to the child. Never, ever, hide things. It will backlash on you later and affect your child adversely, if you evade the truth.

It isn't easy to admit unusual circumstances. So perhaps you can consult a counselor or minister or even a friend that will advise you on the best approach to tell your child something. Just make sure you are honest, sincere and truthful.

Eveline Sandy

Chapter 15: My Uncle's Insight

After my mother's death in 1981, I learned some facts about my biological father.

I had a long conversation with my uncle and he related this to me. My biological father's name was Rolf William. I never met him and probably never will. I don't know if he is alive or dead today.

My Uncle Rolf Behm told me that my mother never told my birth father she was pregnant with me. I don't know the truth concerning my conception. I never questioned my Mom if it was true or not what my uncle told me.

I believe it was a dark part of my mother's life and she wouldn't, or couldn't speak of it to me. After I found out the truth I chose not to cause her undue pain by insisting on an explanation.

Please understand, it mattered to me that Mom didn't tell me I was adopted, but didn't matter to me that Rolf William was my father. Even if I knew earlier in life, I probably wouldn't have set out to find him.

Mom had originally met Rolf William on the eastside. He was well liked by my grandmother, uncles and aunts. No one knows what broke them up. Uncle said Mom didn't tell the family she was pregnant, until after she decided to live in freedom.

I am sure it was a very difficult decision. I don't know how her family reacted to her being pregnant with me and not being married. They probably didn't approve, because of the times, and I can only speculate on the situation she would live through, if she stayed with the family. All I do know is my mother wanted me to be born and live in freedom. She was very young and courageous.

Once I got over the initial shock of knowing I had an adopted Dad I started wondering what Mom went through during her pregnancy. Can you imagine being in a strange land, alone, pregnant and no job?

I'm not sure Mom realized the struggles she would endure by not having her family near during her pregnancy and birth. I couldn't imagine not having Mom near me during my children's births. It must have been scary and lonely for her. It must have been extremely important to Mom that we lived in freedom.

Although I didn't ask Mom directly about the adoption, I did ask about my early years. She told me she made all my clothes, because there wasn't extra money to purchase new ones off the rack. Sometimes friends or neighbors with little girls would give us "hand-me-downs" which Mom greatly appreciated. She was never too proud and accepted them graciously.

She never allowed pride to get in the way of accepting help. Mom believed we were all put on this earth to help each other in love and grace. When she could, she would make little things and give them to people as well.

I am sure I didn't always appreciate Mom's efforts with my outfits. I was more of a tomboy all of my life. I just couldn't see all the fuss with bows and frills, lace and dresses. I would rather be in jeans, tee shirt and sneakers. That's how I am to this day.

Mom would stay up many a night to hand stitch little blouses and dresses for me. Later on in my life, she still hand-stitched material and created beautiful clothing. Her hands seemed to be constantly in use. Mom never believed in "idle" hands. She said it made for the devil's workshop. She taught me well.

No matter how little we had, I never felt like I missed out on anything because I had my Mom's undying love. I could always depend on her. I will miss her to my dying breath.

There are days when I wish I could pick up the phone and hear her sweet voice, but Heaven doesn't do phone connections. Anyway, it would be one heck of a phone bill!

In another conversation with my uncle, I found out Mom and I never actually lived alone in Boblingen, Germany. We seemed to always live in an attached apartment or attic or an addition to an existing house. That probably was good from the safety aspect. The first place was in a quaint little room in an attic over a restaurant. The landlady was Frau (Mrs.) Vaultbower. Mom would go into the restaurant and shyly say hello to the owner. He was very kind to us, and ultimately Mom got a waitress job there.

Uncle used to tell me in German, "*Ihre Mutter Liebt sie so!*" "Your Mother loves you so!"

Mom told my uncle about this event concerning my Dad. Uncle Rolf said Mom never told the few men she dated about my existence. It was the same with my adoptive father. Mom wanted to protect me from anyone she might consider dating.

My growing up years did not include having a phone in the house. It was a luxury we couldn't afford. So if friends wanted to see us they would have to come by, knock on the door, and see if we were in.

One day Michael stopped by our home unexpectedly and asked Mom where I was. Mom said I was in the other room sleeping. He asked if he could see me and Mom agreed. He went into my bedroom where I was and looked down and saw me lying there, turning blue and not breathing! He picked me up and yelled at Mom to get the car to go to the doctor who was less than a minute away in a nearby village.

In those days, doctors generally worked out of their homes and were always available at a moment's notice. The doctor brought me around and had me breathing in no time. He rushed me to the hospital and I ended up being there for three months with whooping cough.

Michael saved my life. If he hadn't had that "feeling" to stop over during his lunch break and check on me I would be in Heaven. My guardian angel, and my Dad, were certainly looking out for me. I believe, at that moment, Mom fell in love with Dad; because of what he did that day for me, when he showed how much I meant to him.

Not long after that, I understand, they were married. The date was September 5, 1955. I was two-and-a-half years old. They were a very handsome couple and deeply in love.

I found a photo of them and another of me in a little halo of flowers and a long dress. I know Mrs. Vaultbower was present and Mom had a beautiful dress on. Dad was in his military dress uniform.

I don't believe any of Mom's German family attended the marriage service. I found out that shortly after the ceremony, Dad discussed with Mom about adopting me. I understand it was an intensive process to adopt a foreign child. After the government approval of the adoption was complete, I got Dad's last name.

Mom and Dad never had any other children together.

Eveline Sandy

Chapter 16: My Dearest Friends

I really loved my job at the bakery. It was my first real job. I was so young and innocent, and the people I met were happy and positive in their personalities. The employees were so kind to me.

I met a fellow co-worker there by the name of Carla. She was also in some of the same classes as me in high school. Carla had a quiet type of personality. She wasn't very outgoing. She was 5'10", slender, blonde, with blue eyes and very pretty. The guys asked her to go out, but she always declined because she was so shy.

Carla worked in the restaurant section of the Hecht Bakery. Her father was the head baker. He was from Holland and was very quiet and serious. He was a very nice man to me. We would work together all week long at the bakery/restaurant.

We would sometimes get so silly and find ourselves in the most laughable situations. There were occasions, because of where the food was served from the kitchen, if one of us turned around too fast with the food, we could collide with another server. Well, one day I picked up a huge sundae and turned and Carla was walking by, also with a tray of food. Splat, we collided. We were both draped in strawberry and whipped-cream sundae syrup and mashed potatoes and gravy. We laughed and laughed. We looked hilarious. The customers laughed as well at our antics.

Unfortunately the owner didn't appreciate it, and deducted the cost of the sundaes and food from our pay. I think it was well worth the laughter!

On the weekends we used to hang out at a Washington D.C. bar to have a drink and dance with the guys. The Maryland area where I lived was a "dry county" and didn't serve liquor. We never went home with the guys, nor gave our phone numbers out. We enjoyed the music and then went to our mutual homes.

The only thing we did that was questionable back then, was we hitchhiked together. Neither one of us owned a vehicle and we didn't always have enough money to take a cab. Back in those days hitchhiking was a bit safer and not as dangerous as today. It was the hippy-times and we all wore bell-bottoms and tie-dyes.

Everyone expected that kind of behavior. We met some interesting people. No one really bothered us. The drivers were very kind, and not a bit lewd, or suggestive.

Carla and I have endured all these years. She is warm and kind and fun to be around. I can feel safe with her and share things with her that I know she won't tell anyone else. She was like a sister I never had. When I needed emotional support, Carla was always there for me. To this day Carla tells me we are closer than her own sister is at times. I have been blessed to have her in my life.

***

A life changing event occurred when I just turned eighteen years of age. It happened while I was at work and hostessing at the Hecht Company Restaurant. Carla was also working that fateful day as a waitress. Two well-dressed gentlemen entered the restaurant and asked me if I knew who Eveline was.

I replied, "What do you need her for?" Then they firmly responded, they needed to talk with her now! In a quick moment I said, "That's me!'

They took me aside and said that I could no longer work in the United States; that I was not a legal citizen. What in the heck were they talking about? Thoughts ran through my head. Wait a minute. My Dad was an American GI, he married my Mom and then adopted me. Didn't that make me an American citizen?

I was shocked and dismayed and scared. Confusedly, I put my hands up to my face and just wanted to talk with Carla and make some sense out of this, but I couldn't. I knew I had to inform my boss, I had to leave immediately.

The men handed me a packet of immigration papers that stated how to become a citizen. Then they left.

I went to my boss and showed him my papers and explained to him, as best as I could, what just happened. I said this would take me about three weeks to study, then I would go to Baltimore and take the citizenship test to become a legal American. He was very kind and understanding and said he would hold my job open for me.

I felt very blessed by my boss's decision, because he knew I was the sole provider of my Mom and myself. I thank God for him to this day.

During those three weeks I had to go to the library to read up on American history and government. I crammed the information in, and found it interesting. However, I found nothing in those books that pertained to everyday life.

What Did I Do Wrong?

I was exhausted by the three-week ordeal. Yes, I was frustrated. I had always thought I was an American citizen and felt like I didn't "belong" once again in my life. I was determined to do what they told me and completed the packet as instructed. Carla, Mom and I went all together to Baltimore, and I took the test.

Yes, I passed the test and went to sit out in the hall while my papers were scored. A man came out, took my hand and said, "Congratulations! You passed. How does it feel to be an American citizen?"

I didn't answer, and then he asked me to come into his office where he swore me in.

Now I felt like I could answer his question. I said, "I thought I was an American citizen already because I have lived here since I was six. My father was an American GI and married my Mom and adopted me. So, really I don't "feel" any different then I did before. Except now, I have papers."

He just looked at me and said, "You're done and have a good day."

All three of us left and went back to our respective homes. I immediately called my boss and went back to work the next day. I had to financially make up for three weeks of lost wages, and it took me about three months of hardship to "catch up".

***

I had another dear friend whose name was Darlene, also from my school. Her father was in the Air Force and her mother was a teacher at a local elementary school.

Darlene had an Amazonian stature. She looked like a model; a blonde bombshell. We went to an Iron Butterfly concert together. She was spotted by the drummer and was approached later by him. I recall they dated for almost a year. Some people…. Ha-ha.

Another time we went to an Atlanta Pop Concert in Darlene's old white hippie clunker car. There were three of us gals; the other girl's name was Jan.

We were driving along, and for some reason all four hub caps popped off on the freeway. We were a sight, running down the freeway to rescue the caps and put them back on.

We went to see Led Zeppelin, Janis Joplin, The Who and other rock groups. We didn't bring any money with us, because Darlene said we could climb over the fence.

As we climbed over the fence Darlene ripped her pants and we were laughing so hard. Darlene said, "We are still going, rips or not. No one will care 'cuz they are either drunk or high." So we went.

We stayed a few days and slept underneath an orange parachute at the festival. People kept approaching us, begging to sleep under the parachute with us. We said, "No way."

On the way home Darlene said, "Enough, I'm tired of sleeping outside. Let's get a motel room. We're dirty, smelly and need showers after being outside for days."

Jan and I asked how we could afford that, and Darlene responded, "I have my parent's credit card. Hurray!"

We said, "What! We didn't know that."

Darlene said, "Well they gave this card to me to use only in an emergency. I think this is an emergency 'cuz I can't stand how we STINK!!"

We found a motel, showered, ate, slept and the rest is history. We had such a blast. Those were the days.

I still stay in touch with her brother, Lou occasionally. Darlene and I haven't seen each other in several years. The last time we talked was in 1999. We each went on with our own lives and still carry good feelings toward each other. I did have more casual friends but these two were my best friends.

It has been a long time since I had best friends for any length of time. We moved around so much, it was difficult for me to maintain relationships.

I came home from work one day and Mom said our neighbors, Sophie and Steve, had invited us to a party. They lived next door to Mr. O'Brien and Mom let them know we would be coming. Earlier, Mom met this guy named Charles Atwood through Sophie and Steve, and Charles was also invited to the party.

Let me add, this was extremely difficult for Mom, to actually have male contact on a dating basis. She still loved Dad intensely, but she also had emotional needs and longed for a man in her life for companionship.

Oh what fun this party was going to be! We hadn't been out for fun in a long, long time. We showered and dressed and went to the neighbors. It was a short jaunt next door for Mom. She was still not strong enough to walk long distances.

Their home was beautiful, and was elegantly laid out. The entryway had wooden, double doors. As a child, I was overwhelmed because the doors looked ten feet tall. At first, I felt out of place, but then I got comfortable because everyone was warm and friendly.

Mom had previously met Charles's son, Chip, and told him she had a baby. He asked if he could meet her at the party?

Mom responded, "Yes, I certainly will bring Evie with me."

The party was in full swing and a knock came at the door and Sophie yelled out for me to answer it. I opened the door and it was Charles and Chip. I had already met Charles and we greeted each other, then Chip asked his dad who I was.

I said, "Hi, my name is Evie."

Eveline Sandy

Chapter 17: First Love

Boy, did Chip look surprised. He said, "Hi, my name is Chip and your Mom said she had a baby. I had no idea that you were my age." He smiled down at me. He was tall, dark, and had short hair which was nicely styled. He had a wonderful smile and oh, so adorable eyes. He was gorgeous.

After a time, we started dating, and we dated for about two years. He was in his first year of college and was very proper. Chip was gentle and respected me. My "red flags" never went up with him. He worked at a gas station and I visited him there when I wasn't working, or going to school. We had a lot of fun together and I suppose it was "puppy love".

What made this whole situation crazy is that Mom was actually dating too. And guess who it was? Why, Chip Atwood's father, Charles.

Charles had lost his wife to cancer several years before. He also had a daughter named Jane. Jane wasn't too thrilled about Mom dating her dad. Maybe Jane thought Mom was going to replace her mom. Of course that couldn't happen.

Charles and Mom were inseparable. Mom still lived at home but spent a lot of her time "wining and dining" with her new love. Mom seemed so very happy, at last. Her illness was in remission, which pleased me immensely.

I was still working and going to school. My immediate goal was to graduate high school. It was grueling, going to school so early in the day, with the travel time between school, work and home. Then I had all the work hours. The time I spent with Chip didn't seem like it was enough. But you know; looking back, it was worth every moment.

Tenth grade was uneventful, except I had one teacher that was a gem. We were in Silver Springs, Maryland, at Blair Montgomery High School, and she was my English teacher. Her name was Miss Naughton, and she befriended me that year. I looked up to her and respected her.

Tragically, she was murdered one terrible night in her apartment. I didn't find out until a general announcement was made by the principal over the P.A. system at school the next morning. I learned later from the news that the murderer killed the wrong person. Miss Naughton lived in a top floor apartment. The murderer was intending to shoot the person in the bottom floor apartment and somehow shot and killed Miss Naughton by accident. What a waste of life.

***

Chip's dad, Charles would take Mom with him everywhere. Charles's family was pretty affluent and lived a higher end lifestyle. Charles belonged to a country club. He introduced Mom to all his friends there. I understand they all liked her and thought she was pretty. Mom just seemed to fit in anywhere.

Charles showered Mom with gifts. She really enjoyed them and had to get used to the spoiling, since she hadn't had anyone in her life treat her like a princess.

I loved watching Mom as she radiated happiness and peace. I thought in my heart, at last, that elusive day has come. She was going to be fine forever. Those years I remember with a smile on my face.

Chip and I continued to date and deepened our relationship. On my sweet sixteenth birthday, Mom and Charles bought me some roller skates. Don't laugh, that's what I really wanted. About the same time, Chip moved out of his dad's home and moved in with a friend of his, Matt LaGuard, and his mom, Ollie.

Chip rented out the basement apartment of their home. Matt said I couldn't spend the night, and that was okay. Chip had thrown my sixteenth birthday party in his new basement apartment.

Chip had also surprised me with an engagement ring, but hadn't asked me to marry him as yet. He waited until later that evening to propose.

After the party we went to our favorite bar in Washington D.C., by the zoo. I had a fake I.D. that got me in. All of his friends were there. After he proposed, they congratulated us, and toasts and hugs were abundant. Life was a fairytale and I felt like a princess that night. I was so in love.

We went to my home that night. Mom was gone to Charles's visiting. This was my first sexual experience since the rape. I was always too afraid to let a male near me. I loved this man so much and wanted Chip to make love to me. Chip thought I was a virgin and I couldn't bring myself to deny that. In my heart I was.

I didn't know how to tell him that I had been brutally raped.. The flashbacks of those men hurting me was still inside of me. This was going to be something I never experienced as a willing participant. Would there be pain and fear involved as I experienced before? I didn't know. Or would it be ecstatic, heavenly and romantic as I had heard?

I had never talked about the rape and the after-effects with anyone. With that thought, how do you tell someone new and important in your life, that you have been raped?

It is important a person is honest and upfront. It is also extremely important for the partner to receive the information in a positive light. Rejecting the person for what has happened in the past to them, is not an appropriate attitude. We were all placed on Earth together to help each other and love each other.

I look back now and wish I would have spoken to someone about my feelings. Trying to be with a man, in a normal sexual relationship is almost impossible after a rape. When I was with Chip, I faked my reactions and Chip didn't notice anything off. Gradually, my barriers lowered and I, very slowly began to enjoy sex.

To this day, I still deal with emotional pain from the rape. Sometimes, the lingering thoughts of despair and uncleanliness come to mind. I want desperately for these feelings of dejection, pain and hurt to go away, but they never do.

I never told Chip about my rape, because I couldn't take the chance of him telling my mom.

The next day we told Mom and Charles we were engaged. We all met at Charles's home. Mom took it okay, but not Charles. He hit the roof. He said that Chip was just too young and still had most of his life ahead of him.

We both listened to what he had to say, and in the end, Chip said he was ready to go and we left. We both were determined to spend our lives together.

I told all my friends at school and work. Carla was so happy for me. I was still working and going to school. Chip and I hadn't set a wedding date yet, and as the year wore on we weren't getting along as well as we used to. Chip was putting up with continued pressure from his father, which confused me, because we were practically family anyway. After all, Charles was in love with my Mom and continued to date her. So, the natural thing would be for Chip and me to be together as well.

One day Chip came to me and said, "Evie, we should break up for good."

I sobbed, "No Chip, this isn't right!"

"No Evie, everything is going too fast. We have school to finish. We are too young. Maybe my father is right."

I didn't know how to respond. My emotions froze. I was being abandoned again by a man. I felt alone. "What did I do wrong?"

I cannot describe the pain inside me. I let Chip go without any further argument. Chip turned and walked away. I sadly watched him, and a part of me left with him. I felt so dead inside.

We still saw each other occasionally, but things weren't the same anymore. We no longer dated. We basically saw each other at family get-togethers.

There were no harsh words ever between us. I just wanted to be left alone. No, I didn't get in between Mom and Charles. They continued to stay together. I was glad and thankful for them. I didn't hold any malice against Chip's dad. Charles was also okay with me. Everything was sad, but okay.

I desired somehow to forget the hurt that I was experiencing from the break up, so I decided to learn and teach ballroom dancing. That was a diversion I needed, and it was great fun.

***

Mr. O'Brien was getting sicker and sicker. We did what we could for him, but unfortunately he finally died. We attended his funeral and mourned for a really kind and generous man.

Some days later his estranged wife informed us she would have to sell the house and we would have to move within a month. I immediately went looking and found a one bedroom apartment for Mom and I to move into.

Chapter 18: Graduation

I didn't actually graduate with my senior class. It was necessary for me to have two operations during the year. I had pilonidal cysts on my tailbone that had to be removed and had to recuperate in bed most of the year.

The majority of my teachers allowed me to make up the work and submit it for a passing grade. The only teacher that refused me, was in science. He insisted I come in for the final tests. There was no way I could attend; I was under doctor's orders. Consequently, I didn't qualify for enough credits to graduate.

I was very angry and almost blew school off and said screw the diploma. I missed my prom and any fun events during my senior year because of my medical problems. I wanted to call it quits. Then I thought about it, and wondered who was I getting back at?

Chip's dad always said to me how important an education was. So I decided not to go to summer school, but re-entered senior year in the fall. I only had to go one quarter, take the test and then I finally received my diploma. I was proud of myself.

School was out for the summer and I went to live with Ollie and Matt LaGuard. Chip had moved out, and Matt's family had the basement apartment available again. I needed to stay away from Charles and stop running into Chip. I was still hurting from the break-up with Chip.

I paid all Mom's bills and she continued to live in her own apartment. In the meantime, I started learning to dance. This was extremely enjoyable. Most of my free time was spent learning and then teaching dance..

I taught it at Pat Patrick's School of Dance. A lot of older people attended there. They actually were fun to be around. They weren't stuffy like I thought my elders would be. They actually welcomed a young thing like me. I felt good being able to get someone to laugh or smile just by dancing with them. We also had a Thursday night class for the handicapped kids. That was especially rewarding and a lot of fun.

Then Matt got interested in dancing. I used to always describe the fun time I had, so he started working there as well. After a short while, we became dance partners. It was truly oodles of laughs. We became good friends and that's all.

I didn't see much of Chip any longer. I still thought of him on occasion, but with regret. Finally I knew it was over. Mom told me "first love" is the most difficult to get over and if anything, it makes you tougher and wiser for the next encounter. I hoped this was so, because it hurt tremendously.

Chapter 19: My Island Trip

I had a close friend, Heline that asked me if I would like to go to the Virgin Islands with her and her sister Rose for three months in the summer of 1971. I told Heline I didn't have enough money to go. She explained to me that we would be renting out a house in St. Thomas and it wouldn't cost that much, because we would split it three ways. So I considered it and thought what the heck; this could be a once in a lifetime chance to visit an island.

I told Mom about the trip and she readily agreed. I made sure all her bills were paid while I was gone. I told my boss I was going to be leaving and that it would do me some good to get away for awhile. I had butterflies in my stomach, because I was so excited about traveling out of the USA again. Heline's sister, Rose, was already in the Virgin Islands and waiting for us.

Heline and I flew together, and we went stand-by, which was much cheaper. We had a layover in San Juan, Puerto Rico, and then took a much smaller plane to the Islands. We arrived and guess what? It was raining! Although it didn't take long to stop, it was still beautiful. It was like looking at a postcard picture, only very real. The people were all so friendly, helpful and kind.

This was the summer after I graduated from high school. What a graduation trip! I was so proud of myself for my progress in life, despite the roadblocks. Gosh, I knew Mom was happy, because Charles would take care of her. I had a feeling in my heart that someday those two would get married. I hoped for an equally bright future for myself.

While I was in the Islands, I wrote Mom every day. I told her how much fun we were having and what we did each day. We went to tan at the beaches, going out at night sometimes, seeing the sights.

At night, we had to be careful because of the natives. I guess some of them didn't like people from different countries coming to their island. They were rude, and we avoided them. Today it is very different on the Islands.

When we were at the beach we would take photos and they would hold towels over themselves so we couldn't snap them. It was bad "juju" to have their faces photographed. I think they were a very superstitious people.

I didn't have any worries in life and things were very relaxing. We didn't intend to go to the Islands to date or find guys, but rather just wanted to get away and enjoy life. Three months went by so very quickly. Then it was time to go back home to reality.

St. Thomas, Virgin Islands

Chapter 20: Reality Check

The trip back to the States, from the Islands was uneventful. When I arrived at the terminal gate, Mom and Charles were there to pick me up. Mom looked me up and down and said what a great tan I had, and she loved my color. We stopped for lunch and I showed them all the photos we had taken.

Well, I started life over all fresh and new. I looked for a different job, and anticipated making some new friends as well. I decided I needed something more challenging in my life.

I applied for a waitress position at a bar. The bar's name was "Act 4."

Heline and Rose went there quite a bit and knew the band. Heline said no one would bother me there, because she knew everyone and it was a cool crowd. I wasn't old enough to work there, because they served beer. I used my fake ID though, and got the job.

I tried it out and made some spending money the first night and gave Mom some.

One night when I was waitressing, I was talking with some folks and I got introduced to a gal by the name of Belinda. She was from Germany too. We were chatting in German and English and it came up in the conversation that I wished I could find a better job making more money.

Belinda said she co-owned a massage parlor and needed a receptionist immediately. She said she would tell her partner I was her cousin from Germany and I was sure to get the job. She would get back to me in a couple of evenings.

I discussed the possibility of a new job with my Mom and she told me to be extremely careful, but I was old enough to decide what I wanted to do. I didn't want to stress Mom too much about this opportunity I had, but I really wanted the position.

During this time, Mom still went in for check-ups and she still remained cancer-free. Hurray! Praise the Lord! I felt relieved about that.

Belinda got back to me within a few days and said I had the job if I still wanted it. I said yes. My duties were to answer phones, do filing, and set appointments for the masseuses. It was an easy, but busy job, and I made excellent money. I always sent money to Mom out of every paycheck. She was very thankful for that.

Charles did not support my Mom, nor live with her. They maintained separate residences, although they had a great companionship together. I don't think my Mom allowed their relationship to go further, because she still hoped for my Dad to return.

I couldn't live in the basement any longer. I moved into one of the empty rooms at the parlor. At first, it was acceptable to me, but I didn't stay there very long. It seemed Belinda and her co-owner, Phillip, were having an affair and they met at the parlor for their dates. Belinda suggested I move in there so she wouldn't have to see him so often. I agreed reluctantly and said it would only be for a short time. I felt manipulated by Belinda, but I couldn't just quit, because I had too many responsibilities.

Chapter 21: Phillip

One day a man walked into the parlor where Belinda and I worked. He was average height and had a swimmer's body. He had dark, wavy hair, and was handsome and very charming.

Belinda introduced me to her co-owner, Phillip. He lingered by me and I guess he liked what he saw. Belinda didn't mind his interest, so we started a whirlwind romance. We dated for about four months. He was courteous and respectful to me and introduced me to all his friends.

I suppose that was a measure of how important a relationship was back then or even now. That is, when a person introduces their love interest to all their friends, whether to get the friends' approval or to see if the love interest fits in. It is a given for both adults and young people.

So, presuming that statement, if you have dated a person, say about three or four times, and they haven't introduced you to at least one friend, you might want to question if the dating is going to go to the next level. If the friends don't even know you exist, then I would seriously question how important you are to the person you are dating.

We went to a lot of nice places and he always treated me like a lady. We traveled all over the States.

After dating for a while, he asked me to quit working at the parlor and move in with him. By the time he asked me to move in, I was already in love with him and said I would think about it. I wanted to say "yes, yes, yes!" but I always talked out any of my major decisions with my Mom first.

Mom finally had a phone in her home, complements of Charles, for the first time in her life. I called my Mom as usual with the news, and she responded, *"Liebchen*, you're a big girl, just be careful and think first. I'll always be there for you, and back you up, whatever your decision."

I loved my Mom so much for the support she gave me, and she was always available, day or night, to talk with me.

I called Phillip and eagerly said, "Yes!" He was older than me by fourteen years, but I honestly overlooked that. I believed I was a bit more mature than my age, because of the experiences I had been through.

We got along well together, and after a while he wanted me to go to bed with him. I didn't respond. Instead, I asked him about our future together, and he said it looked very promising and that he was in love with me. He then said he wanted to marry me someday. We left it at that.

I still maintained friendships with Carla, Heline, and other friends. I told them about our plans and they said they were all happy for me.

A few weeks later, Phillip asked me again if we could go to bed together. I figured, because we were in love and had a commitment, it was permissible. We did, and this was my second experience since the rape. After we had sexual relations, a weird feeling came over me. I blurted out, "Phillip, I think you just made me pregnant!" Phillip said I was absolutely silly; no one knows that instantaneously.

I wasn't silly, as it turned out. As the days and weeks went on, I was nauseated and tired and not feeling very well. Phillip said I should go to his doctor and see what the problem was. I set the appointment up and Phillip went with me. Well, it wasn't a problem or disease; I was pregnant. The doctor came out to Phillip after examining me and shook Phillip's hand and said, "Congratulations, you're going to be a father!"

What a time for this to happen. I had very mixed feelings. I was glad, but scared, but I didn't know what to think or how to tell Mom.

Phillip, on the other hand, was ecstatic. He reassured me that he was happy, and slowly I accepted his happiness as well.

Not long after that, Phillip told me he wanted to go visit his mom in Florida, and instead of inviting me along, he said I should go and stay with my Mom for awhile. I asked him how long he would be gone and he responded he wouldn't be gone very long.

I didn't think anything was wrong; I was three months pregnant and still very nauseated, so travel would be difficult for me.

I called Mom and asked to come home for a short time. We still maintained the one bedroom apartment and I could use one of the twin beds. Of course she said, "Yes, *Liebchen*, come and stay with me."

Mom didn't have to ask Charles about it, because she never moved in with Charles, although they were still seeing each other. She always hoped and prayed Dad would return to her. He was her one true love of a lifetime. She never found out why Dad left her, or even when he left her.

I suspect Dad wasn't a very strong personality, and he couldn't endure the long term illness that Mom had. He didn't have the guts or stamina to stick around.

Anyway, Phillip and I said our good-byes and I packed a suitcase and went home. Phillip would call me every day, sometimes twice a day, and he was gone for a total of two weeks.

He returned from Florida with a whole new attitude though. Someone spoke to him disparagingly, about our unborn child and Phillip's commitment to me. When he came by my Mom's home, I had already packed up my things to come back to him.

He drove up and started making excuses and told me it would be better if I got an abortion. I screamed at him that it was too late for that. Why didn't he want this child? He handed me money and I took it and hid it to be used for the baby's support later on. He ignored my questions and simply said it would be better if I would stay with my mom a bit longer.

I retorted, "I don't know who it would be better for, Phillip." We argued back and forth for a bit and I reluctantly agreed to stay with Mom.

He continued to call daily. During this time I babysat for a friend, and Phillip would come to visit me. He didn't offer money to help me. He made no attempt to hug or kiss me. It was a bit strange. I tried to talk about the baby to him. I asked, "Are you going to change your mind? Are you going to be involved in our child's life?"

He unemotionally responded, "I gave you the money for an abortion. What do you think my answer is?" I think I almost hated him at that moment.

I couldn't understand why he kept calling me and visiting me at my job. It didn't make any sense to me. The "bit longer" turned out to be four months later. I was then seven months pregnant.

He drove his Porsche to my mom's home, I thought to pick me up, to talk with me about our child and our future. Maybe he had come to his senses, and he wouldn't leave me to raise our child alone.

So I got in his car and he didn't start the engine. I asked why? He said he wanted to talk with me first. He said, "I'm sorry Evie. I am not ready for marriage or fatherhood. I cannot do this."

For a moment, my heart went down to my feet. I couldn't say anything, because I was so devastated. Here I was carrying his child. He handed me a $20.00 bill and asked me if that would help?

I was crying. "Help what? You couldn't buy a layette with that. Why are you doing this?" I grabbed the money and ripped it into pieces and threw it at him.

I jumped out of the car, as best I could and ran in the house sobbing. He drove off and I never saw him again.

I couldn't believe anything anyone said to me anymore. I had reached deep inside me to trust this man. This man was the father of my unborn child. This man had played my emotions. He was fourteen years older than me. What did he mean he wasn't ready? How could he not be? He wasn't a young kid!

Oh, I hated him at that moment. I got out of his fancy car and didn't look back, because there wasn't anything worth looking back at. What a piece of work that man was.

I saw Mom looking out the window and knew she saw the tears running down my cheeks. There was one person I knew, who always loved me.

I opened the front door and Mom knew something was very, very wrong. She held out her arms and said, "*Commens sie hier, meinen liebchen.*"

I flew into the safety of her arms sobbing. She comforted me until I calmed down enough to talk coherently. I told her everything and I kept saying "What am I going to do, what am I going to do?"

Mom, in her usual way, hugged and kissed me and said, "Everything will be alright, Evie. Truly."

Chapter 22: Life Decision

I wish with all my heart that life was easier than it was. What exactly did I do wrong? I gave my heart, my body, my commitment, and it was thrown back in my face.

My tenacious trust with men was getting thinner and thinner. Most of my downs in life were all related to men. These men were my biological Dad who abandoned my Mom when she was pregnant, my adoptive Dad, Jeaneen's father, Uncle Donald, the beasts that raped me, Chip, and now Phillip, who abandoned me when I was pregnant.

My mother's history was repeating itself through me. My heart was broken. These men always left me stranded and emotionally wiped out, even when they professed they loved me. I didn't know where to begin to trust again. I wasn't sure I could.

Later that fateful evening, Mom and I sat down to talk seriously about my baby who hadn't arrived as yet. I asked Mom what I should do. Give the baby up for adoption? Raise the baby?

I felt I didn't have anything left to offer my baby. I had no home with a husband, no job, no money and I was emotionally spent.

I considered an adoption, even though I was really torn about it. I wanted to give my child every chance at a good life, with a mother and father that loved my baby. Having all of the advantages of a good home was most important to me. It would break my heart to give up my baby, but I needed to put aside my emotions for the good of my baby's life. I just didn't know if I had the strength to do that.

I was faced with so many decisions to make alone. Should I do the best I could and give him or her all my love, and hope everything else would work out?

I was so very torn up inside from Phillip rejecting me and rejecting my baby; his baby; our baby. My self esteem was at its lowest.

All I knew for sure was I loved the child within me and wanted to keep her/him close to my heart. I wanted to shower all the love I had inside me on that child of my spirit.

I used to talk to my child within my belly, reassuring her/him of my unconditional love and commitment to protect her/him from the outside world. I wanted my child with me; I needed my child with me. I loved my unborn, eldest child so much. I felt I couldn't breathe without my baby, my innocent child, my little peanut.

I just felt so incapable of providing a good life for my child. I didn't want her/him to go through the same tragedies and rejections I endured. I volleyed back and forth everyday, trying to figure out that I wanted the best life for my baby. That's why I seriously considered adoption for many weeks.

I felt a family that had a mom and a dad and all the right elements for a good strong future would be the best life for my unborn child. Truly, considering this would further break my heart. But, my love and selflessness would insure my child's future. I didn't know how I would survive the separation of a lifetime, but it didn't deter me from considering adoption if it was best for my child.

Don't think for one moment this was easy for me. It was the most heart wrenching decision I would have to make in my lifetime; deciding what to do about my baby.

The most important responsibility a person can have is to raise a child, and there are no prerequisites for employment. You don't have to go to school, get a license, or get a degree. You don't even have to be an adult. As soon as you have a child you're expected to grow up, make all the right decisions and teach your child all the right things in life. Insanity!

As I said, I thought about different avenues for some time, and Mom and I talked again and again about my options. Mom said if I decided to keep the baby, she would help me in any way she was able to.

She said she would support any action I took, but it was solely my decision. I believed her more than anyone in the whole world. She was my rock. She never purposely let me down.

Through all this, I learned a difficult lesson. I didn't trust easily anymore and I became very careful about letting anyone close to me. At this moment in my life, I had to put everything in perspective and carefully consider any situation before I made a decision.

Here's another episode in my life that I had to endure in order to survive. I had definitely matured. I made my decision.

Soon, I went to my Mom concerning my decision on what to do. I decided on keeping my baby and do the best I could. My Mom was so happy, she started crying and hugging me. She said 'my grandchild' that, 'my grandbaby' this... She was going to be a very proud *gross mutter*.

Mom kept saying everything would be fine. It would be hard at first, but my baby was worth it, father or not. Mom and I always made it together. We were strong together.

I realized what Mom went through when she was pregnant and without the father in her life. I also know through Mom's experience, it made my situation a little easier.

Well, I was eight months pregnant and couldn't find a job. I got the opportunity to baby-sit for a girlfriend's child. I made a little bit of money; not much, but anything helped. Deep down inside my heart, I was still hoping and praying that Phillip would call. I never heard from him again.

Each day seemed a little easier as I accepted my situation. My resilience to life prevailed and I stood on my own two feet again. Even so, this confused nineteen-year-old brain still wondered if men could stay committed to women. I'm not sure I can even answer that today.

During my pregnancy I still visited my friends and went out with them on occasion. I really didn't have any interest to go, but they always included me, so I felt obligated.

My special day was getting closer and I was getting more and more afraid. I really didn't know what to expect.

During visits to the gynecologist, I didn't ask questions and didn't receive a lot of medical guidance. I was big and cumbersome and felt like a small elephant. I was tired all the time and breathless.

I remember Charles would drop by Mom's and when I couldn't bend over to shave my legs, he would do it for me, up to my knees. Truly, he would have made a decent step-dad. He was a good man and he wished I could have done more in life.

He didn't judge me for the pregnancy either. He was always into education and felt everyone should go to college. His daughter went to Duke University and later married a professor. Chip also went to college.

Carla was also always supportive of me. She was an excellent friend to have. Being pregnant wasn't a joy ride. I was laughing one minute and crying the next. I felt like I was on an emotional seesaw.

With the little money I managed to save up, I bought a small layette for my new precious arrival. I purchased some clothes for a little girl and some for a little boy. In those days, the medical technology didn't provide the ability to find out the sex early.

One evening, Charles came over to Mom's and said I could go over to Ming's restaurant with them for dinner if I liked. I gladly accepted the invitation. The only problem was, I didn't have a lot of decent "pregnant" clothing to wear, so I wore the same old dress that I always wore.

I guess I looked fine; I was just a big, round ball in the middle. So off we went for the evening. When we got there, at first I was feeling so-so and then Chip showed up with one of the girls from the dance studio. It was Nora of all people. I just couldn't believe my eyes. Here was my first love with that bimbo!

Don't get me wrong, I am not usually judgmental; it was because I hadn't seen him in a long time and it stunned me that he was with her. I have to admit, it hurt too. I don't think a person ever really gets over their "first love." I was pleasant enough, although I would have loved to choke Nora. Humph.

While we were still at the restaurant, I excused myself and called Carla. Carla asked where I was, because the lady next door was giving me a surprise baby shower. (I never went out in the evenings since I had gotten so big, so of all the nights she picked, it had to be that one.)

I went back to the table; everyone was finished eating, and I asked Charles if he would take me back home. I explained the reason why, and even though he was drinking, I was hoping he would still give me a ride. I had told Carla I would be there as soon as possible.

Unfortunately, it turned out to be later, rather than sooner. I finally reached home and thought that Carla and her friends had given up on me, and I started blubbering. Charles was a good man, but sometimes his drinking was overwhelming to say the least.

While I was sitting on the couch crying, I heard a knock on the door with Carla on the other side saying, "Come on Eve, stop crying and come with me."

I went with her and I was surprised when we entered my neighbor's house and all my friends were sitting there, smiling, laughing and yelling, "Surprise!"

I didn't realize, until then, how many great, supportive friends I have. I got oodles of gifts for the baby and even the cake was scrumptious. I even got a bassinet, which I really needed. I thanked everyone and told them I was so happy and getting more excited as each day went by.

I only had a few weeks to go, and then I would hold my precious child in my arms.

> *Love Never Dies*
> *Oh my child, please come to me*
> *So I can hold you in my heart*
> *Let me protect you from the world*
> *Let me treasure your small arms around me*
> *Let me always listen to your words*
> *Allow me to witness your achievements*
> *Allow me to comfort you in defeat*
> *Accept my strength and my courage*
> *To help you face your difficulties.*
> *Take my undying love as armor,*
> *Take my heart, tear it to pieces,*
> *I will never turn from you,*
> *My child, my love never dies for you."*
> 2009-mg

My blessed friend, Carla, came over one day and handed me a portion of her savings. She wouldn't let me refuse the gift and told me I would need it in order to start out on the right foot with my little one. With tears in my eyes, I hugged her and thanked her.

What a wonderful person Carla is. I still keep in contact with her to this day. We have been lifelong friends for more than forty wonderful years.

I could always talk to Carla and Mom. Mom never thought of anything bad, when I used to get upset about anything, and start ranting and raving, as I called it. Mom would wait until I ran out of steam and then give me a hug and say, "I love you so much, *mein liebchen.*"

Those hugs sure made things seem less harsh. I loved her so very much. I used to tell her that a lot. She was a great parent as well as a friend.

Dear reader, remember, the last time you say, "I love you," to your child, spouse, parent or friend, could be the last time they hear it from you. We never know when we are going to leave this Earth. So always take the opportunity to express your love. Always!

Chapter 23: Enter Christopher Thomas

January 15, 1973 was my special day for the birth of my child. Early in the morning, I wasn't feeling well. I felt over-bloated and sore from lower back aches and general icky. I told Mom, and she said I'd better call a taxi and we would go to the hospital.

I also called Carla. She said she would be over as soon as she got off work. The taxi came, and Mom and I were off. Now I really was feeling a sharp, rolling, aching pain across my midsection. I was getting more and more scared. We arrived at the hospital, got out, and I lumbered into the hospital, up the elevator and into the maternity area.

There were no wheelchairs to ride; in those days you had to walk. It felt surreal. This was not a dream, it was real, and soon I would have my baby in my arms.

The doctor examined me and said I was only dilated to one centimeter and would have to go to ten centimeters before I could have the baby.

The doctor said I would be there all day and they wouldn't let me go back home. 'So this is what labor is like,' I thought. 'No wonder they called it labor; it sure is'.

When I didn't have the rolling pains, the time passed slowly and I was bored. I didn't think to bring anything to do because I really didn't know how long it would take to give birth.

I heard the doctor say to my mom that if I didn't have the baby soon I was going to have to have a C-section. Wow, I didn't want that, so I started praying fervently, "Oh dear God, please let me have my baby naturally. I don't want an operation that could take weeks and weeks to recover from. How could I possibly support my baby and myself if I was laid up for too long?"

The staff came in and hooked me up to IV's to calm me down, but also to induce labor. That baby of mine just didn't want to come out into the world. The pains were getting worse and worse, wrenching moans from me. I knew it couldn't be much longer; I wasn't even sure I could take much more pain. It was a grueling eighteen hours of labor.

All of a sudden, the staff came, I gave Mom a hug, and they took me from my room into the delivery room and transferred me to the bed in the middle of the room. They told me to start counting backwards and put a mask over my face for the pain. I didn't want a lot of drugs, even though the pain was bad, because I really wanted to see and experience my child's birth.

I don't remember all the details. I think a mother has temporary amnesia so we don't remember the excruciating labor pains, or else we would never want to get pregnant a second time. Ha-ha. I do remember the doctor saying, "It's a boy!"

My son weighed eight pounds and was as healthy as a horse. The doctor placed him on my chest. Oh what a wonderful feeling it was, having that sweet child, that was all mine, who I would love unconditionally forever. His name was Christopher Thomas, and he was so small and cuddly and smelled so good.

They let me have him for a short time and then took Chris to the nursery to be further cleaned up and fed. Afterwards, the staff took me out of the delivery room and into the hallway, where I stayed on the stretcher for a short time. They then returned me to my room. Soon, it was time to go where I could see Christopher again through the nursery window. He looked so beautiful.

My Mom stood at the window with me and was wearing an 'It's A Boy' button. She told me that when she looked at Chris, he knew she was his grandmother and gave her a big smile. Mom said it was one of the greatest days of her life, except for when she had me. I stayed in the hospital for about one week, which was the custom in those days.

Then, it was time to bring that bundle of joy home. It was difficult at first, being a new mother and all, but I had the best teacher in the world with me, my Mom. The weeks flew by and I knew I would have to go look for work soon, or we wouldn't be able to pay the bills.

At the time, I was receiving welfare and food stamps. Since Mom was living with me, she wasn't able to receive anything, although she had military medical coverage. She received no other pension. I didn't like being on welfare, but I had no choice at the moment.

When Chris was three-weeks-old, I found employment at a nationwide taxicab company, as a phone operator. Unfortunately, the only way I could get employed was to tell them my son was six weeks-old.

In those days, a mother wasn't allowed to go back to work until six weeks after her baby's birth. It was fantastic to earn a living again and get a check every week without having to rely on anyone else for support. We had a roof over our heads and food in our stomachs.

I enjoyed going out and buying things for Chris and Mom. Don't get me wrong, I didn't fritter away the money on needless things. I was very thrifty and could make a dollar go far.

Mom would always thank me for my generosity. It was a satisfying feeling to know I was appreciated for what I did.

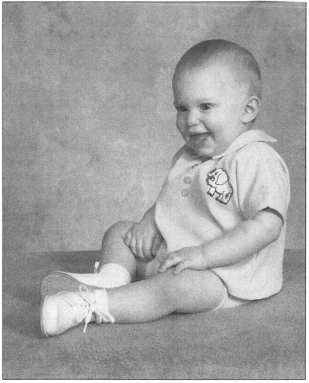

1973 - Chris at 9 months

Eveline Sandy

Chapter 24: Life Goes On.

I got a promotion of sorts from the national cab company to work at an affiliate that was also a courier service. Once again I was a telephone operator. My phone style and voice were outstanding, so I soon advanced to become the head telephone operator.

This wasn't the happiest time in my life, but I was content nonetheless. I had my baby, my job, and my Mom; life was complete. I wasn't interested in dating or going out. Mom said I would be a boring person if I didn't go out every now and then. Taking care of a household was a great deal of responsibility and my young-adult years would soon slip away.

I do admit, the pressures seemed overwhelming at times, but I would remind myself of the brighter side of life and I would smile. Life slipped into a routine.

Mom continued seeing Charles, and she was happy. They had seen each other for several years, and Mom loved Charles dearly. They were great companions and friends.

She would always tell me how much Dad still meant to her and he would always be in her heart no matter what. You could ask any of the people who knew Mom, and they would say that she never spoke ill of her absent husband.

When it was time for me to get home from work, Mom and Chris would be standing by the window, waving at me. He would get all wiggly and excited when he saw me walking up the sidewalk.

Chris was eleven-months-old for his first Christmas. He was already walking. He loved putting on *Oma's* red shoes and shuffling around the apartment. His first Christmas was very cold, and it snowed all day. We kept each other warm; we had each other, our little family. It was all worthwhile.

Santa brought little pull toys for Chris. Chris went wild; he would drag those little toys around all day laughing. He was a happy child.

Just maybe the ups and downs of life were behind us. We didn't have to move around anymore. There were no more drunken stupors from my father and no more yelling. There was just glorious peace.

Chris's first birthday was a party. Mom made a cake and we put a party hat on all of us. He sat in his high chair and we took pictures of him playing in his cake. He was a chubby, happy little boy, my son. That year went by quickly, as did the next few years.

My jobs changed. I went to another courier service where the same boss owned Central Delivery. He sold it and started a new company. The owners asked me if I would consider moving out of state, to Arizona, to work for them.

At first, I was speechless and told them I would seriously think about it. I decided that it was time for a change in my life, for the better. Maybe all that moving around when I was younger affected me with wanderlust.

There was a complication though. Sometime after I had Chris, I met a guy by the name of Kenny Reed. We dated for about a year, and we were going steady. I allowed him to meet my mother and son, Chris. I had the same attitudes about having my dates not meet Chris like my Mom did with me. It seemed like a good rule to follow to protect the little ones.

Kenny was a good-hearted person. He was always thoughtful and caring and never cruel to anyone. We were getting more and more serious about each other and spent a lot of time together. I remember meeting his delightful parents and visiting them at their home.

After he met Chris, they got along well together and we took Chris over to Kenny's parents on Halloween to Trick-or-Treat. That was the first time they met Chris. They seemed to like him and like me as well. As they got to know Chris and I more, they wanted to know when Kenny and I would get married.

There's a sad side to this. Kenny had been married before, for quite a few years, and he was legally separated, but not divorced. His "ex" refused to sign the divorce papers.

The laws were different back in those days and without her co-operation he couldn't become divorced. There was nothing he could do except wait. I prayed his "ex" would change her mind. There wasn't a reason that I knew of to cause her to hang on to Kenny. He wasn't in love with her and didn't live with her, so why was she doing this?

I hoped this would be resolved before I made the decision to move. Kenny and I discussed my job offer, and he told me to do whatever would be better for me in life.

I really didn't want to leave my home in Maryland and all my friends, which included Kenny. We shared some good times that will never be forgotten. My dear Kenny was always kind and considerate. My memories of him are positive.

Kenny had sons of his own and he was proud of them. I met his sister and brother, and liked them instantly. I wish sometimes we could have had a future together. I prayed that I would make the right decision when it came to the move.

I knew it was time to move on. His wife wouldn't let him go, so what could I do? One day I met with Kenny, told him my decision and said good-bye with a tearful, "Hope to see you one day again."

Kenny told me that the day his divorce was final, he would call me and let me know. He said there was one thing though, and that was that if I ever wanted to go out, not to feel guilty, because I still had my whole life ahead of me and he couldn't promise me anything. He didn't know how long before the divorce would be finalized and he could be with me again. He would not ask me to wait for him. Initially he called me on a daily basis and even came down and visited me once. I felt really loved.

I gave my affirmative answer to my boss concerning the move to Arizona. It was in October, 1975. The existing company was sold, and some of the employees stayed to work in Maryland. The rest decided to relocate to Arizona with the new company. That was great because I had instant friends.

The southwest seemed so far away from the east coast. It was like another country. The desert, the weather, the mountains, even the people were all so different. I was nervous about the move, even though I moved around so much in childhood because of Dad and the Army.

We packed everything we had. This time we had accumulated a lot through the years, so we had to get a moving van. We paid for the van, although the boss paid for our plane fare.

I was ecstatic, because Carla was going, too. By this time, she was married to a real nutcase by the name of Fritz. Fritz and I didn't get along with each other. In my opinion I am glad they didn't have children together, because it could have been disastrous for them.

Carla was my best friend, and I naturally tried my utmost to be nice to Fritz. Unfortunately, he was very hostile to me and controlled Carla's every move. And I mean every move. If she didn't obey him, he would beat her. I would see her at work and she would have bruises on her arms.

It broke my heart to see her so banged up, knowing he did it to her. He told her never to have anything to do with me. Carla couldn't give up our friendship so we still talked at work, for which I am thankful. He apparently not only hated me, but felt intimidated by me, because I encouraged Carla to report him to the authorities.

One day I went to work, and Carla wasn't there. She never called in sick, because she was a workaholic and never missed a day. Every morning, without fail, we had coffee together before work, so where was she?

All kind of thoughts went through my head. Did Fritz kill her? My heart was thumping; I was so scared. Was she in the hospital because he beat her up again? What did she do wrong in Fritz's eyes this time?

Carla didn't have a phone, so I couldn't call her. I didn't have her home address, because Fritz wouldn't allow her to give it out to anyone, especially me. I had her parent's phone number but couldn't contact them during work hours. I thought about it, and felt I was thinking the worst. I calmed my thoughts and prayed for her.

The second day arrived and still no Carla. The panic of not knowing filled me again. I asked the boss where she was and he responded she hadn't called in sick and he hadn't heard from her.

Later that evening, I finally spoke to her parents and found out they bought her a plane ticket and she returned back east to them. What a relief to me, knowing she was alive and safe and wouldn't be beaten again.

Periodically, I called her to see if she was okay. She lived at her parents' home for several years. I know it took her a long, long time to recover mentally from Fritz's abuse. The conversations were short and basically I just wanted to reassure her I was there for her.

Carla and current spouse - Bob

Finally, it was time to move. We all, about eighteen of us, went to the airport and said goodbye to Maryland. We took a red-eye flight, and because we slept, it seemed like a quick trip. Soon we were landing at Sky Harbor Airport in Phoenix, Arizona.

Linda Parker, an Arizona-based employee, picked us up. She was just an acquaintance then, but soon after became one of my best friends and ultimately one of my bridesmaids, at my first and only marriage.

Eveline Sandy

Chapter 25: Home-Based in Phoenix

One of the perks of our move, was my company would pick out an apartment for us. They paid the first month of rent and after that, I was responsible for the bills.

It was the nicest home we have ever lived in. The complex had a swimming pool, air-conditioning, and a closed-in area so Chris could play and not wander off. I didn't understand why air-conditioning was standard, but it was because of the extreme heat in the "valley of the sun."

Arizona natives say it's a dry heat. I never quite understood the meaning of that term, because hot is still hot. I always lived in four seasons and not in a Summer/Autumn type of climate.

Even though Mom's health was improving, she still couldn't work and had continual setbacks from all the medical damage to her body. She didn't have any income and only had medical coverage from the Army. We were adjusting to the new surroundings.

I was so lonely. I suppose that was expected. I left behind a lot of good and bad memories. I left behind Kenny.

Mom left Charles behind as well. When Mom moved with me, Charles moved to Jacksonville, Florida, to retire. He did call Mom often, to see how she was doing. He was always a presence in her life.

I was very determined to stay and make Arizona my permanent home. It was difficult for me, because I was in survival mode for so much of my life. I felt this was an opportunity to now put down roots and give Chris security, so he wouldn't have to move around like I did and experience the trials of life that I did. I have lived in Arizona for over thirty-five years.

Over the next eighteen months, time flowed quickly. My boss arranged to rent me an old, yellow Ford Fairlane for $15.00 a week, and the insurance was included. It was great to have transportation to get back and forth to work and to run errands. Chris was growing up fast and Mom was maintaining her health. But the feeling of slight unrest was continuing to grow within me.

One day I went to visit Linda and her brother, Tony, was there. He said, "Hey beautiful, I think I have a blind date for you." I said no, as usual, but Linda said " I'll protect you, go ahead and go."

I continued to refuse, but between Linda and Tony they finally convinced me. They would bring up things like, "This guy is cool. He doesn't smoke, doesn't drink, and doesn't do drugs. What more can you ask for? Come on, Evie, give him a chance, go out with him."

Something inside of me said go ahead and go, enjoy yourself for once with the adults. So I did and I met Donald Sandy.

Chapter 26: Donald Sandy - My Man for Life

Tony and Linda arranged for Donald and I to meet at their home one evening. I arrived and waited in the living room, then sat down on the sofa, fidgeting. I impatiently waited for the big moment. A knock came to the door and Linda answered it. Linda led Donald to the living room.

Wow, wow, wow! This was one handsome cowboy. I was speechless. Linda introduced us and Donald said, "Are you ready to go out, Evie?"

We had prearranged that Tony would go with us, to get us over the rough spots of getting to know each other. I got up and we left in his truck. We drove around and stopped at a local biker bar and had a beer. We laughed, and carried on and listened to the music. They both drove me back to Linda's home and Donald thanked me for the evening.

We dated a short time. It was a whirlwind romance. I was filled with butterflies whenever I thought about him. He swept me off my feet and I felt like I was floating on clouds.

You know how you feel when you fall head over heels for someone? Every thought turns to the person you are attracted to. It doesn't matter if you are eating a ham sandwich and you wonder if that heartthrob likes ham, or you wonder where the future will take you two.

We spent all our free time together. We would go for long drives and talk and talk. He was so interesting. He would tease me and we would laugh a lot. He seemed really interested in what I had to say as well. He was a fabulous slow dancer and we would dance for hours. He would hold me close and his breath was heavenly in my ear. His touch was strong and comforting.

Our first kiss swept me away in emotion. The whisper of his lips touching mine ever so gently, persuaded my lips to part. Donald held me firmly in his arms, like he never wanted to let me go. My eyes were closed and my senses were whirling.

Thoughts were drifting slowly through my head. I felt warmth filling the center of my body. I had never felt that way before.

Was this the taste of things to come? I wanted more. I wanted him. I wanted him for a lifetime. I felt like the kiss lasted forever, but it was only seconds. It was extraordinary. I fell in love.

I wished the kiss could have gone on forever. As I look back, I wonder how those first kisses disappear. I wonder why romance disappears and ordinary life events prevent a couple from carrying on with the romance of the "First Kiss".

Perhaps we should all look back and make sure we keep those feelings alive within a marriage or relationship. You still love each other, but where are the "fireworks?"

As we dated, I felt more grounded with Donald. I didn't feel he would abandon me. I didn't have the tools to overcome the fear of my past, but eventually I continued to feel more and more comfortable. I felt our souls were merging together, as we were becoming one.

It was time for Donald to meet Mom and Chris. I felt a bit of nervousness and prayed everyone would like each other. This man in my life would soon be joining my family, I hoped. It was extremely important to me for everyone to be happy. I wanted my son to finally have a loving father that he never had. I wanted Mom to approve of my choice of Donald.

Even though I was in love with Donald, I had to put aside those feelings of love, so I could make a practical, logical decision to move ahead with this relationship. I didn't take my decision lightly to have Donald become my son's step-father. I couldn't just ask Christopher, at age four, if he wanted Donald to be his dad. He was too young and had no control over life's decisions. I was solely his guide in early life; his teacher, his provider, his mother.

I prayed to the Lord for discernment and grace to decide correctly for the future. My Mom was a great judge of character and instantly like Donald. Chris responded positively to Donald's attention. He wasn't used to having a male figure around. I thought this was really going to work out!

The next thing I knew, Donald proposed and I said yes, and we were getting married. He told me he loved me with all his heart. This was the absolute happiest I had ever been.

It was April Fool's Day, 1977, that we met, and I was the happiest fool around. I think it was instant love. I finally had a man in my life forever and ever; a man who was caring and interested in the true me. I was his, and he was mine. It was an extraordinary feeling.

It's amazing to me how people fall in love and then feed it, so it grows stronger and stronger like a tree in sunshine. It takes endurance as well as commitment. Communication is absolutely a necessity. It is puzzling to me when people can stay together for an indefinite amount of time and not kill each other in the process.

You have to have a mix of mutual trust, love, and friendship to start and maintain any relationship. Add in respect, honesty and patience as well, to know you are staying together for your lifetime, through every situation, good or bad. That is incredibly scary. It is only by the grace of God that you are able to face all the trials and all tribulations that this life brings in front of you. None of us knows what tomorrow will bring.

What is that extra portion that makes a relationship last? Is it resilience? Is it knowing your mate will always be "in your corner," fighting for you and not leaving you no matter what s**t hits the fan?

Can you tell me the perfect fool-proof recipe for a perfect marriage? I would really like to market it. You will find out, no matter who says otherwise, there really isn't an exact relationship recipe.

***

We set our wedding date for July 17, 1977. I wasn't nervous or reluctant. I knew full well this was the man I wanted to spend the rest of my life with. I was serenely happy.

Here this tall, 6'1" lanky, handsome man stood, ready to take me as his own. He had brown short hair, brown eyes, thin lips that didn't smile much, but did he have a sense of humor. He would say the funniest things and have me bent over in fits of laughter. He was so gentle and loved Chris and Mom as well.

At moments it didn't seem real; that long, lasting love finally arrived mutually in our hearts. We were meant for each other. Was this the way Mom felt about my Dad when they first met?

At first Mom wasn't happy about the marriage. Maybe it was because someone was coming into our lives that could replace her. I don't think she realized she could never be replaced in my eyes. She was my Mom.

I understood her hesitancy and assured her no one could replace her. I knew she was also concerned I could get badly hurt again, but in my heart I knew Donald wouldn't do that to me. Mom and I discussed this before the wedding and I must say Mom handled this situation in a very maternal way. We loved each other so, and there was room for one more in our lives: her future son-in-law.

Don and Eve's Wedding

The big day arrived. I was so nervous and could hardly think coherently. Donald hadn't seen me since the night before; it was the superstitious practice of the groom not seeing the bride. The day dragged on, and the preparations were wearing me down. Why did we pick an evening wedding?

Finally, the time arrived and the last moments of our single lives began. Sammy, Donald's brother-in-law, escorted me down the aisle. Linda was my maid of honor. Donald's best man was Ronnie. We had the services in the back yard; it was cowboy wedding in honor of my Donald. His brother Gary made a full size cowboy poster and had bales of hay and matching red long-johns on the clothes line. There was also a keg of beer and food and down-home country music. It was a dream come true and I remember that day oh so very well.

Donald had Levi's on, with a dark-blue cowboy shirt and hat and western boots. I wore a cream colored, high-waisted, lacy, floor length dress. It fit me perfectly. My hair was long and I had rolled it during the night so it was full and sparkling. Chris was dressed like a miniature cowboy and my mom wore a peach, short-sleeved floor length dress.

When I walked through the kitchen out to the backyard, it seemed like it was taking forever to get to my Donald. I remember the look on Donald's face when he spotted me. The love shone in his eyes and a big grin was on his lips.

We made a great looking couple, if I may say so. After exchanging our vows, we stayed for a short time, thanking everyone for the great wedding party, then off we went on our honeymoon. Yes, we had an actual honeymoon. Whoo-Hoo!

One thing happened that confused me at the time. My mother-in-law came up and hugged and congratulated me and whispered in my ear, "You didn't only get Donald, you got the family as well."

I didn't get it at the time. Now I do.

I gave Chris a kiss and said bye to Mom, who was taking care of him while we were gone. We went to Prescott Valley, Arizona. It is a great getaway, about two hours outside of Phoenix.

There were no vacant motels so we found one just on the outskirts of Prescott. It was the first night together, for the rest of our lives. It was romantic, and oh, making love was so wonderful.

The next day we drove up to Flagstaff, and Donald found some kind of unknown type of plant. We found it at the parking lot of the Grand Canyon. He plucked it and put it in his hat. Later we found out it was a marijuana plant so we quickly got rid of it.

Exploring and discovering new things with someone by my side was a strange and wonderful feeling. We tired ourselves out exploring and headed back to Prescott and chose a different motel. Donald took our baggage out of the car and put it inside of our room. This room had two double size beds, (like we needed that), and a kitchenette with large arcadia doors.

We were exhausted, and decided to shower and go to bed immediately. This room was kind of strange because of the cooling/heating system. One side of the room was hot and the other side was cold. There was no consistency.

The night before we had shut our suitcases and left them on the other bed, and now when we came out of the bathroom the suitcases were open. That was scary; someone apparently was in our room during the time we were showering and they were checking out our belongings.

We did go to bed, but didn't sleep soundly. Early the next morning we gathered all our things and noticed my hair dryer was missing. Donald thought I left it at the last motel but I didn't.

I had long hair and made sure I always carried my hair dryer with me. I was quite upset but we didn't go to management. We didn't want to further spoil our honeymoon with complaints, forms and alibis.

We agreed we would never go there again and we didn't. The rest of our honeymoon was good, without any other misfortune occurring. It felt like we were in our own little world and nothing else mattered; at least for the moment.

We decided to go back home early and start our life together, since we still had some time off from work. We just lazed around, doing the usual honeymoon things folks do.

At the end of August, I had a conflict at work. I was an early morning shift-supervisor. A fellow employee was having problems with her supervisor and wanted to switch shifts to mine. The two of us went to the head supervisor and presented the situation. We presented the problem low-keyed and professionally.

She said, "If you don't like the way things are run, just quit."

At that moment, I felt the lowest of the low. I couldn't understand what her problem was. All I could figure out is that she had a bad day.

I went home and poured out my heart to Donald. We decided I should quit in September of the same year from the courier service. I went back to work in a couple of days and my supervisor never once apologized. Later, I quit as planned. I enjoyed staying home, being a housewife and a mother for a change. I think Mom appreciated it as well, seeing she was Chris's constant caregiver, Granny.

One week after Donald and I got back from our honeymoon, I received a fateful call. The caller was Kenny. He said the divorce was finalized; all the conflict was over and he saved some money to have me come back to Maryland and stay with him. There was no discussion of marriage in the conversation.

One of the most difficult conversations I had, was to tell Kenny I had just gotten married. I told Kenny that Donald was very special and I was in love with him. I reminded Kenny that he told me to move on and if by chance I was free when he got his freedom then we would plan for the future together.

It was wonderful to know Kenny still cared, and I told him I cared for him, but now as a dear friend and always would. We tearfully ended the conversation, wished each other well and hung up. I buried all the memories of him deep in my heart. Through the years I have never regretted my decision to stay married to Donald; he is a "keeper."

Around Christmas time, Donald and I decided to look for a two bedroom trailer to live in. We quickly found one and then had to find a space to put it on. Donald's parents made it all possible by co-signing for us. We were thankful for that assistance for the future.

Donald's parents came from Oklahoma and moved to Arizona for work and to better themselves. They were married young, fourteen and twenty-one, and they were married for fifty-three years. They had six children: five boys and one girl. They are Gary, Kay, Ronnie, Donald, Terry and Karl. They weren't a huggy-kissy family, which was weird to me because we were.

I called his dad, T.J, instead of the usual Dad or Pop. He was a big equipment mechanic, and I remember his dirty finger nails. He couldn't get them clean, no matter how much he scrubbed.

He was tall, with an average build and had fine, straight, gray hair. Donald was a "spittin' image" of his dad, although Donald has a much warmer personality. T.J. was a very stern, nonemotional man who could stop the grandkids in their tracks with a quiet roar of two words.

He revealed little of himself, but was quite good with the "Twenty-Questions" game with the grandkids. He didn't intermingle much with them though. He left that up to his wife.

Donald's mom's name was Rose. She was a stocky, big-boned, medium-height woman. She had salt and pepper wavy, thick, hair and wore glasses. She was introverted and would talk one way, but later say something else behind your back. I am not indicating she was mean, it was just her way.

Rose loved to cook. She encouraged anyone that came in to eat something. If you said no, she would keep asking until you ate something, then expect you to have second helpings. The grandkids loved her and were always around her.

Basically, the whole family lived in the same trailer park, except for Donald's brother, Gary. Donald's granny lived in the trailer behind his parents. He didn't like her, because he felt she was mean. I liked her, although we didn't say a whole bunch of things to each other.

Donald's parents' front room in the single-wide had a homey feel, with one couch and a recliner. When we had family gatherings, the men hung around in there watching television. The ladies would be in the kitchen, chatting and eating.

I never felt a part of the group, because I don't think we ever gave each other the chance to get to know one another. I tried to fit in. Even though I was outgoing, I felt uncomfortable saying certain things. I think I was afraid I would be judged negatively.

I don't ever go into anyone's house and go into their refrigerator or pantry, even if I am invited to. It is not my way. So consequently, I would get served food, but would do without a drink, unless I brought my own from home, because everyone else got their own. I suppose, because of my isolated behavior, the in-laws probably thought I was snobbish and different.

Even though I didn't feel accepted by most of the in-laws, they were nice to my Mom. Also, Donald's parents and my Mom were cordial to each other. Mom went to most of the get-togethers, even though she had a strong accent and wasn't always understood. She was willing to join in. All the nephews and nieces called me Aunt Eve. That made me feel warm and accepted inside. I belonged.

***

We were so excited to move our belongings from the apartment to our very own trailer. Super-Eve thought she could move most of our things herself. So I dropped off Donald at work and I got busy.

What a project! We owned a short-bed pickup truck. (Who doesn't in Phoenix?) I managed two loads and gave up. Finally, Donald got off of work and took over. It took all day, with about four trips total. It was one cold day in October.

Don, Chris, Eve

    We had to stay at Donald's parent's home for two days to prepare everything at the trailer. Donald installed gas pipes in the ground because we didn't have any when we moved the trailer to the space. It took six weeks getting the city inspections approval. In the meantime, we had to run electric heaters. Yes, even in Phoenix, in winter, it gets a tad cold. No matter what problems arose, this was our house; our home.

    Mom liked our trailer a lot, it just wasn't very large. It was only a two-bedroom. We had bunk beds in the second room for Mom and Chris. Chris opted for the upper bunk, so Mom could be comfortable in the bottom bed. We were all happy and content.

We spent Thanksgiving at Donald's parents. It was uneventful and each of us pitched in a dish. At Christmas, we picked out our first tree together as a family and hauled it back home in that little ole pick-up truck.

We had Tony over for dinner a lot and Donald would be so relaxed and in a good mood. I loved seeing him that way. Tony was a sweetie to my Mom. He used to say to her, "Susie, you can say anything you want. I love listening to you." And Mom would just chatter away to him. I don't think he understood half the time what she was saying. It was too funny.

Then we hadn't seen Tony in quite some time because he got busted for drug possession. He got involved with the wrong crowd. So consequently, he was spending some time at the facility in Florence. I was glad he was temporarily out of Donald's life, because Tony tended to be a bad influence on him.

I was torn though, because Tony was such a good friend to Donald and we really missed his terrific, outgoing personality. Donald was the only person that took the time to get under Tony's layers of B***S*** and understood him.

Our home was our sanctuary. I had sewn curtains for it and took pride in decorating on our scant budget. It was home.

Chapter 27: Enter Jesse Lee Sandy

It was January, 1978, and Donald and I talked it over about having a baby together. We weighed all the pros and cons. It was going to be expensive to bring another child into the world.

Chris was old enough to be a big brother, we had our own home, and I wasn't working, so all the signs were positive to go ahead. The pros outweighed the cons so we agreed to proceed.

We made a doctor's appointment and went in to have my I.U.D. removed. We were told it could take months before I got pregnant after having an I.U.D. Well, one month later I went to the doctor and got a pregnancy test and it read, "Yes, preggers!"

Boy, I was sick, every single morning. I had the same symptoms as the pregnancy with Chris. Somehow I thought things would be different. Hah.

I'd raise my head off the pillow in the morning and say to myself, "Okay cruel world, is it time to get up and puke again?" Actually it was okay, because I knew within months I would have another sweet bundle of joy in my arms. It was all worth it.

Chris and this little one would be six years apart in age. I prepared Chris about having a sister or brother soon. He was very emphatic about having a little brother only.

I kept my figure this time, and didn't get that small elephant look quite as soon. Donald was the happiest man around. You couldn't keep the grin off his face.

One day, I caught Mom looking out the window, eyeing the gas man inspecting our new gas lines. I said, "What a nice looking man, Mom. Would you like to meet him?"

Mom said, "Oh Eve" Then she blushed and said, "Yes, I think so."

So, brave little ole me went outside and called out to him and introduced myself. I asked if he happened to need a house cleaner. He said, "Why, yes I do, as a matter of fact."

I introduced him to my mother. His name was Lee Ben. He hired Mom on the spot and Mom was pleased as anything, because she had a job and didn't have to live with us anymore if she didn't want to.

I was so proud of Mom. She would call and tell me what a nice and kind man Mr. Ben was. He had a house full of kids and Mom liked his older daughter, Patty.

Patty had a sister that was mentally challenged, named Tina. Mom said it had to be difficult to be the mother of that household and carry on your own life as well. I met everyone in the Ben family and introduced Patty to Donald's single brother, Terry, hoping they would start a friendship, but they didn't get along. Then Donald's other brother, Ronnie, met Patty and they ended up dating for about one year.

And, guess what? Ronnie proposed to Patty, she said yes, and they got married. They are still married and it's been more than thirty years.

Mom kept cleaning for the Ben's, but then she started not feeling well. I insisted she go see a doctor, so we went out to Luke Air Force Base. Even though Dad wasn't with us, Mom still had medical coverage because of Dad's retiree benefits.

Doctor Erickson checked her over and said she had arthritis of the hip. I asked him to send for Mom's medical records from Washington, D.C., so he could understand her cancer history. He said yes, he would, and I believed him.

Dr. Erickson either didn't send for Mom's records, or simply didn't receive them. He never followed through. He treated her with aspirin to help relieve the chronic pain and gave her little else. That went on for a year.

Finally the pain got so severe, Mom went back again and begged for something else to be done because the aspirins weren't helping her.

Finally, a CT scan of her spine was ordered, after one year of pleading with the doctors to do so. We found out from a medical person checking the file that a wrong diagnosis was made for Mom because lab reports got mixed up from another patient. When the correct diagnosis came back the prognosis was not good; her cancer had returned in full force. This time she had developed cancer of the spine.

I cannot imagine the amount of pain Mom endured that year. The spine holds all the body's nerve endings. My poor mother must have been on fire with pain. God, what next?

This was a very difficult time for me. I was so torn up inside. I used to pray, "God, can't we just have a few good years of peace before we get struck with catastrophe again? Why always us? What did I do wrong?"

I stood bravely by my Mom's side. Because it took so long for the diagnosis, the cancer had spread extensively. She was immediately scheduled for treatments that would continue for a long period of time. I would take both kids and Mom to the hospital two to three days a week.

We would spend six to eight hours a day there, waiting for Mom to get through her treatment. She would come home extremely weak and not able to eat. I felt so helpless.

Next, the doctors informed me that Mom would have to go to Texas for chemotherapy treatments once a month. They didn't provide that specialized treatment here in Arizona. Mom would be at the Texas hospital for two weeks at a time and then come home for two weeks. Mom had no choice but to agree.

This was tearing me up inside; it was another separation. Donald was so understanding with me during my crying bouts of despair. I was so emotional because I was pregnant. I thanked God I had him there by my side.

Despite my joy at being pregnant, I found myself worrying quite a bit about Mom, my best friend for life. Even though she wasn't feeling well, she was happy at the thought of being a grandma again. Donald's family was happy as well.

Months flew by and Chris was preparing to enter kindergarten. I remember the first time I put him on the school bus. I kissed him, told him have a great time and obey the teachers. I felt that sinking feeling in the bottom of my stomach. My dear, eldest son was embarking on his educational journey. Wow. Needless to say, I cried all morning.

Every day, I walked him to the bus stop, and when the school day was over I would be at the bus stop again to greet him. Chris would come running off the bus, school books in one hand and big smile on his face. He would just chatter about his day and what fun he had. I was glad he had adjusted so well.

During the latter part of my pregnancy, I thought maybe someone in Donald's family would give me a baby shower, seeing this would be Donald's first child. Surprise, they didn't think of it and I didn't get one at all.

One day Donald's mother and his sister Kay came to our door while Donald wasn't home. I let them in and they had two unwrapped gifts and threw them on the table. I was shocked and asked them what they were doing?

Kay, with her hands on her hips, said in a snotty tone, "We aren't giving you a shower because we know 'something' about you!" They wouldn't tell me what it was, so I asked them to wait until Donald got home from work in a few minutes. They agreed and sat on the sofa. Everyone was quiet and patiently waited.

When Donald came home I was already in tears because I didn't know what they were implying. Donald walked in the door and saw me in tears and asked, "Eve, what's the matter with you?"

I looked at him, took a breath and sobbed, "You need to talk with your mom and sister."

Donald turned to them and questioned, "Mom, Kay what's going on?" They didn't respond so I sniffled, "I'm not getting a baby shower!"

Kay shouted in a high-toned voice, "We know something about Eve, that you don't know!"

He looked over at them and said, "What could you possibly know about Eve that I don't know? She's my wife!"

Donald didn't appreciate their tone and firmly told them to explain themselves or politely leave. No one was going to slander his wife, especially in our home. One of them, I don't recall which one, said the only reason I married Donald was so Chris, my older son, could change his name to Sandy instead of remaining as Behm. I couldn't believe what I was hearing. Donald turned to me and said, "That is absolutely ridiculous!"

Inside, I thought I was stuck in a nightmare and was willing myself to wake up and all this nightmare would evaporate. I opened my eyes and nope, this was real. I didn't defend myself; I was too shocked to respond. I'm not sure what Donald said after that except he told them to leave our home. They left abruptly.

I went to Donald and hugged him and told him how special he was to me. He was my friend, lover, partner, and a good listener. Donald looked back at me and said, "I'm sorry my family has this attitude about you. I know it's not true. I love you."

I felt so relieved. Donald, in those days, always understood me. We loved each other so much. It took a long, long time to forgive my mother-in-law. I am sure Kay started that rumor because she disliked me and her mom believed her.

At night, when we went to bed, I would lay on my side with my big, round belly pressing into his back so he could feel the baby kicking. Donald would love watching my stomach bounce around. We would sit together on the couch and he would just stare at my stomach watching it go this way and that. The baby was getting so big. I looked like I had a huge bowling ball attached to my midsection.

I couldn't see my feet, and I couldn't shave my hairy legs. Ugh. I waddled like a duck, and I felt very unsexy.

Donald was always there to support me and tell me how beautiful I was and that he loved me. That meant so much to me. Donald was a man of few words, so when, and if, he said something, he meant it. I had to listen real close sometimes.

During this time period, Mom wasn't really sick yet. She enjoyed seeing me pregnant again. She was always there for me as usual. My time was getting closer; my due date was sometime in mid-October.

The doctors were wrong though, Jesse didn't arrive until November 25, 1978, on Thanksgiving Day. We went into the hospital during late October and early November on false labors, thinking it was better safe than sorry.

Donald and I signed up for classes to prepare for our baby's birth. Donald's work schedule kept changing, so he couldn't attend all the classes. So the ones he missed, his mom went with me, reluctantly.

What a change from the last pregnancy; I had a husband to experience this with. Time flew by and I was full of energy the day my second baby came into the world.

We were supposed to have holiday dinner at Donald's parents' home, but I started feeling some really strong pains that morning. Again, we headed to the hospital. I went into the delivery ward and was told I was dilated to one centimeter, which was too small, and to go back home until the pains got stronger and more regular.

The staff said it could be a few more hours or a few more days. Oh, wow. Well, instead of going all the way back home, we decided to follow the doctor's advice, to go walking. So we went to the parking lot at "Pic' N Save" and walked for quite some time...

It felt like I walked three football fields. Donald's mom was with us so we walked pretty slowly, like ducks. We got tired, so we went back home again after dropping off Nanny Lee at her home. We decided not to enjoy turkey dinner at their home because we knew this was the day!

I still had this strange amount of energy, so I cleaned the house. Finally, towards the early evening I started feeling very ill and the labor pains were getting stronger and more consistent. We left for the hospital again, when the pains were about five minutes apart. Mom stayed home to take care of Chris. This time I would probably stay in the hospital.

Donald grabbed my suitcase to take with us. We arrived at the hospital and they checked me and said it was for real this time. As I was getting prepped, Donald left to make a bunch of phone calls to let everyone know that it wouldn't be long before our child came into the world. I changed into a hospital gown and the staff gave me an enema. Oh what fun!

I went back to the labor room and they checked me to see how many centimeters I was dilated. I was restless and didn't want to stay lying down in bed, so I was allowed to get up and waddle/walk.

Every time the rolling pain grabbed my midsection, I would lean on a wall and do the breathing exercises we had practiced in class. That really helped me. I was proud of myself that I was handling this labor so much better than the labor with Chris' birth. Of course it was my second child and they always say the first child's birth is the most difficult.

I told the nurse, I thought I would go and lay down, because the pains were getting stronger and closer together. Donald was constantly right by my side helping me through it all. My mouth was getting dry from not having anything to drink and having to pant when I worked through the pain.

Donald got me some ice chips and fed them to me. I was checked again and they called Doctor Bruce to come. When he arrived he checked me and said, "Just a little longer, Evie."

Somehow, I remember I saw him eating pizza. He walked back into the room and said, "Evie push." Next thing I knew, the baby's head was crowning. Dr Bruce told me, "It is time, Evie!"

I had my bed moved into the delivery area. Donald ran to change his clothing to the protective gown and scrub hat and came back by my side. What a fantastic coach he was. He was always concerned and had a smile of 'love you, honey' on his face. He said he would do anything to take the pain away. What a great man.

The staff scooted me from one bed to another flat surface. Ugh. Doctor Bruce yelled once more, "Push Evie."

I did, and it wasn't enough to expel our precious bundle of joy. Dr Bruce asked Donald to go down to where he was, so he could see our baby being born. Then, Doctor Bruce said, " Push hard Evie."

I did and out the baby popped, after the shoulders moved around. It was a baby boy! A beautiful, healthy baby boy. I asked if he had all his fingers and toes. Donald laughed and said seriously, "Yes Evie, they're all there."

Donald was grinning from ear to ear. He was so proud; he came around the table to me and gave me a lingering kiss and told me he loved me. That's what I missed out on with Chris's birth; the companionship and sharing with a husband.

Donald said, "We need to name him." We decided right then and there, his name was Jesse Lee Sandy. He weighed in at 9 pounds, 3 ounces. He was our big boy. The nurse placed him on my chest for me to hold him. Oh, the love that filled me. He was so healthy and beautiful, thank God. I was complete.

The nurse took Jesse to get cleaned up and took him to the nursery. In the meantime I was getting sewn up. Jesse was a big one, so there was a bit of tearing. I told the doctor I felt like walking to the nursery from the delivery room. They said okay, and Donald walked with me, my arm linked through his. Jesse, who was all cleaned up and dressed in a blue gown, was fast asleep. Everyone in Donald's family was standing at the nursery window, staring at that little, sweet babe. Donald went down the hall to use the phone to call my mother and said I was doing well and her newest grandchild was also a baby boy.

I missed my Mom being at the hospital and I know she would have liked to be there, despite feeling ill. I had asked a few family members to take care of Chris while I was in the hospital, but no one would, so unfortunately she couldn't go.

I have tried to be generous and forgiving in my feelings, but the truth is my Mom and Chris spent Thanksgiving alone at our home and no one checked in on them. Of course they were all at the hospital, not caring that my side of the family mattered.

Donald brought Mom up later that evening. Nanny Lee was still there. The two grandma's gazing at their grandson was so special. While Donald and I were at the nursery window, this man came up and said that there was a baby in there that looked a month old. Donald said, "No way, that's our baby, and he was just born!"

He was just one big baby. At that moment, I felt my life was complete. I had a husband, two sons, my Mom and a home. I was truly satisfied and blessed.

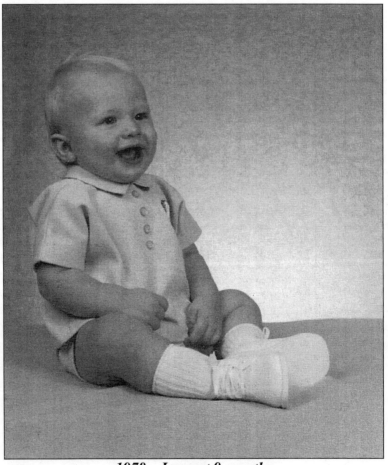

1978 - Jesse at 9 months

Donald had a younger brother by ten years. His name was Karl. The two of them were like night and day in personalities.

That kid, and I mean just that; kid, put me through Hell that I will never forget in my whole life. All he would do is cause problems. I was the target of his abuse. I cannot figure out why he hated me so much; I don't believe I did anything bad to him.

I think he absorbed bad things about me and disliked me for it. I can't prove it, nor do I want to. I felt things would get better, but my patience and positive outlook on life sure wore thin at times. My faith never wavered and my hope never diminished during this trying time of my life.

God help us, but Donald and my son Chris know what I am talking about. I never understood why this child didn't like my son either and had to cause him so much grief and pain. Chris would come to me extremely upset and ask, "Mom, why does Uncle Karl shout at me? He says, 'You aren't a Sandy, you are a Behm, and you don't belong in this family.'"

I would grab my son and hug him and tell him he was loved by both me and Donald. I assured him no matter what anyone said, he could hold his head up high because he was special.

I thought some more and I figured that Karl was jealous that his brother was doing so well as a husband and father. Karl certainly had his own challenges, but there was no doubt he was loved by his parents.

Karl would hit Chris every chance he got. Then, problems arose when he found out I couldn't do anything physical to him, because the authorities would take me away instead of him, even if he was tormenting my child.

He was five years older than Chris and the abuse started when Chris was five years old. I would scream and holler at Karl to stop and at times just plain beg him to leave us alone. Nothing worked, and I mean nothing. I tried cajoling, threats, bribes, you name it, and nothing would entice Karl to stop.

To me, he had an undiagnosed psychological problem, that no one was helping him overcome. There were times I would go over to his mother (my mother-in-law), but she didn't seem to want to listen to anything I had to say. It was like talking to a wall.

Her dear, beloved son was perfect, nothing was wrong with him, and I imagined that he picked on Chris incessantly. His mother said children do quirky things in their life because they're children and not like adults. This kid's actions were totally unreasonable. He put sticks in the spokes of Chris's bike so Chris would fall off and get hurt. Karl would grab a two-by-four and hit Chris for no reason at all. Karl was dangerous. Needless to say, these childish attacks caused a lot of problems in our lives.

I would pray to God and plead, "Why more challenges? Give me a break, dear Lord. I have been through so much. How much more testing or character building do I need? I'm dealing with Mom's cancer, raising a family and now this?"

One day Chris and I were walking over to Penny and Terry's home and saw Donald's brother-in-law Sammy from across the street. I called out hi and he said hi back.

We continued walking, and Karl appeared out of the blue and starting smarting off. He grabbed me around the arm and threw me on a nearby car. He was a stocky boy and a lot bigger than the other boys his age in the neighborhood. He got in my face and hollered, "I'll do more to you."

It ran through my mind there wasn't a physical thing I could do, because he was a child in the eyes of the law. My son Chris ran home and luckily his dad was there and told him what was going on and that I needed help, fast. Karl kept shooting his mouth off as I saw Donald coming down the road toward us. I felt so relieved to see him.

Donald grabbed his brother by the scruff of his collar and looked into Karl's face and snarled, "If you evvver, and I mean ever lay another hand on my wife again, you will not be on this Earth for long. Got it?"

Donald dragged his brother to his home, but not before he smacked him. That was the first time I ever saw Donald hit anyone. Donald knew his parents weren't home so he had to take discipline into his own hands.

Truthfully, I felt relieved. I was always put down by the family, saying that I was imagining the things that Karl did. He was considered "the-perfect-little-boy-that-didn't-do-anything-wrong." I was hoping for the day when someone would wake up and realize Karl had a major problem. I am glad it was Donald that first realized the jealousy issue was very, very serious.

Chris and I went home and I was so overcome with emotion, that I laid down for a while and just bawled my head off. I finally slept for a short time. There was nothing more said on that episode, but the abuse continued down the road.

***

I was broken hearted that Mom was cancer ridden again. It was unbelievable to me that a person who was so good, always considerate, and had a good ear for listening, was ill again. Mom would do what she could, with what she had. I could sit for hours and analyze why, and not come up with any plausible answers.

My faith in God was tested at times. There were so many unanswered questions floating around in my head. There were times I was so overwhelmed, all I could do was cry.

Oh yes, I remember the old adage that the good Lord doesn't give us any more than we can bear. Sometimes I wonder about that statement. I also know in the deepest recesses of my soul that, that is true. I believe thoroughly God has my back. All I have to do is ask for his grace and protection. I am a worthy example of that.

Mom stopped cleaning Mr. Lee's house because of her illness. She had no income, so we asked her to move back in with us. I could feel we really needed each other's love and support. Donald agreed wholeheartedly, because he also loved my Mom. We were family.

Love for people is so wonderful to feel, because it is the one true emotion that God directed us to express; a Godly kind of love.

We all have that gift. We just have to decide on how to utilize it. And that means anytime, anywhere, no matter how tough the road appears. Possessing material things are nothing compared to having a person's love, respect, and admiration.

Eveline Sandy

Chapter 28: Mom is Losing the Battle

Gosh, it seemed like doctors and nurses were a standard part of my life. We had endured this battle for two years running. Mom was getting much worse. She lost her glorious hair and couldn't keep any food down. The cancer had traveled to her stomach.

When I cooked for everyone, Mom could only tolerate liquids. It was extremely difficult eating in front of her, knowing she wanted to taste the food, but couldn't swallow it, or it would come up.

There were times I would make bacon sandwiches and Mom would chew on the bacon for the flavor and later spit it out so she wouldn't stress out her esophagus with more vomiting. I am sure it was disheartening to exist on liquids only, but Mom never complained. I could look at Mom and see the lines of pain throughout her face, along with her smile.

She always said, "I am fine and I am going to be alright, my dear children," while hugging us. "I'll be around for a long, long time. I fought this before and I will do it again."

My two sons knew she had cancer, but didn't treat her any differently than how grandkids treat their grandparents. I was so relieved that they didn't tiptoe around her. Ours was a pretty normal household, with normal boys.

Chris and Jesse expressed their love for *Oma* (familiar form of Grandmother in German) in their unique, boyish ways. I think it helped Mom forget her pain when they included her in their pranks. *Oma* needed their love and ours to go along the long, rocky road ahead.

***

It was vacation time for the kids, Donald, and me. We arranged for Mom to stay with Donald's mother, Rose, for the time we were gone. I admit, while we were enjoying our vacation, I still thought about Mom a lot and how she was doing.

Mom felt like she was an added burden, staying with Rose. She also knew she wasn't able to live alone, even for a few days, and it would ease my mind if she was with family. Mom still wanted to go home, so we shortened our vacation and went back home. No one minded. We were done having fun fishing.

We went to Rose's to collect Mom and it was like *deja vu*; it reminded me of the time I saw Mom, when she first had cancer at Walter Reed Medical Center in Washington, D.C. I remember she was standing at the top of the stairs and wearing a green dress.

All kinds of emotions went through me. She had lost considerable weight that time around and I suspected in the back of my mind, she might not make it through. I wondered then, what was ahead for all of us. Now I know.

About a week later, we got a surprise visit from Mom's cousin and her husband from Germany. It was unbelievable, because we didn't think we would ever see any of our German family in America.

Mom was so tiny (she was fifty-two pounds when she passed on) that they hardly recognized her. She didn't look or feel well. The morphine medication wasn't helping alleviate the constant pain. We all did have a wonderful time together hugging and kissing, eating a yummy meal and sharing our love. Mom looked so happy and at peace.

We sat around the kitchen table and chattered on and on in German. At intervals someone would translate into English for Donald and the kids so they could join in.

Donald said it seemed like Germany was in his home. Everyone enjoyed themselves immensely. These were special moments we would remember with love and heartache.

It was difficult to say goodbye. Everyone knew this would be the last time Mom would see her German family.

Time marches on, and Mom was steadily going downhill. She was getting smaller and smaller, a former shadow of herself. She had to be admitted to the hospital at one point, because her skin was turning yellow in color. She took more tests and the bad news came back that the cancer had now spread to her liver. There was no hope for survival.

Mom bravely asked the doctors how long she had, and the reply was three months, six months if she was lucky; it would be a miracle if she lasted a year on this Earth. There were no guarantees about the elimination of pain, though. The cancer was eating up her digestive system.

I have researched the subject of cancer and discovered that when cancer is in the reproductive organs, radiation and chemo are necessary to completely destroy the disease from that area of the body. It also destroys the good cells along with the bad. Depending on where the cancer is and what stage it has been diagnosed, the cancer is apt to spread to the digestive organs and surrounding areas.

I understand the cure can be more painful than the actual disease, but it is necessary to have the treatments. My Mom never told me of the pain she was in; I could only detect it by looking at her eyes. She was a brave woman to endure that.

My Mom maintained she would have a lot longer on this Earth than the doctors predicted. After all, God makes that decision for us. She did have to stay in the hospital for a short time and I would go and visit her every day.

My next door neighbor, Kathy, had a sympathetic ear for me. She was a kind and understanding person, and I took comfort from her. She had a lot of her own responsibilities, including raising her two young sons. Her husband had passed away years before.

I cared for her immensely and lost contact with her, when she moved away. Kathy would go and visit Mom with me in the evening. I was determined to go everyday and it wasn't always possible to go alone.

People are brought into our paths for a specific reason and a season and sometimes it's not our choice when they leave, or if they stay in our lives. We never know if it is for yourself, or the other person. It is God's plan.

It was getting closer to Christmas. I was torn up by my lack of Christmas spirit. I was worried about Mom, but joyful about my sons and husband. We all wanted Mom home for Christmas. This could be her last so I spoke to the doctors.

They were not very supportive of my request, but after pleading continuously with them, they finally relented with a condition on how to bring her home; I had to learn to give her injections of pain medication, which was morphine at the time.

That stopped me in my tracks. Reluctantly, I told the doctor I needed a little time to think about it. All kinds of thoughts went through my head. Would I give her too much, too little, or would I hurt her on the injection site? There were no clear answers.

There was only one that could direct me and decide for me: the good Lord. So I went to the hospital chapel and got on my knees and prayed for the strength to do what Mom needed. At first, the prayers didn't seem to work, but the longer I concentrated, the stronger I felt God's presence. I felt at peace and knew the Lord would guide me in taking care of Mom.

I left the chapel and went back to the doctor and said I was ready to learn how to administer the shots to Mom and take her home for the holidays. He was surprised at my new found confidence and pointed to the head nurse and said, "Go talk with her and she will show you how."

After explaining to the nurse what I wanted, I asked if I would have practice time on an orange and syringe and she sternly said, "No. Your first injection will be on your mother."

I was nervous and my insides were jittery when she told me. I knew I could do it though. I knew the Lord was holding my hand, keeping me steady, that I could do this and not hurt Mom. I almost fainted!

After a couple of minutes I was okay and it wasn't as difficult as I thought it would be. I swabbed her hip with alcohol, then uncapped the syringe and sprayed a bit to clear the needle of air and gently jabbed it into Mom's hip. She was smiling and didn't wince at all. Mom did say it felt better from me than when the nurses gave it to her. I loved her so.

The great news was Mom was coming home and there were no more problems from the doctors. I packed up what Mom had at the hospital for our journey home. It is hard to describe how wonderful I felt inside. I actually made it possible, with God's guidance, for Mom to come home.

I held Mom closely in the front seat of the truck, all the way home. When Donald and I settled Mom in, she looked so much better and happier than at the hospital. Chris and Jesse went wild, hugging and kissing her, dancing around and singing, "*Oma's* home, *Oma's* home from the hospital."

Mom was beaming. Her grandsons were her world, and her eyes sparkled with happiness for them. We had lots of tears but more laughter; that was our household that night.

"I am not giving up." "I have too much to live for." "I'll always be here for you all." "God will care for us."

My Mom asserted these statements over and over again to me and my family. She always had a positive outlook and never once admitted defeat, despite her weight loss, her pain, and her lack of strength. She carried a lot of faith.

My Mom was truly the role model of inner strength, hope and love. She had an endless amount of patience to give, more than most people would ever imagine. She was the rock of our family.

She was pure of spirit, never tried to hurt anyone intentionally and innocent of the bad things in life. She simply would not allow evil to affect her. She gave me the wings to learn how to fly. Have I told you I was truly blessed to have a mother like her?

At night, when it was time to get her shot, she would quietly whisper to me, "Evie, I need my shot, honey. I'm sorry to wake you up."

I knew it wasn't the schedule she was concerned about, but the pain she was enduring, and that the morphine would dull the pain, so she could sleep. She was sleeping more and more; slipping away from life. She was hardly eating at this point.

***

Christmas arrived; there was no snow, but hey, we're in Phoenix! This was a sad Christmas, knowing it was probably Mom's last and still, we had to make it joyful. I did the holiday shopping for Mom, since she only moved from the couch to her bed and back.

She didn't have much body strength anymore; the cancer was robbing her of it. Mom purchased some wonderful gifts for the boys. We also gave Mom some gifts and she was so happy to receive them. We got her bright colored nightgowns.

There were two kind ladies from Hospice of the Valley that helped me with the care of Mom. Their names are Bee Stephens and Micki Schaffer.

Among all the tasks hospice offered, one of them that was most crucial was, if I didn't have enough gas, or money for gas, to transport Mom to the hospital, those lovely ladies would alternate, taking Mom to doctor's appointments. They would call daily to ask how Mom was doing, and how I was doing.

They also came by for regular visits to check in on Mom and see if she needed anything at all. They even supplied a sheepskin to put under Mom's sheet to allow her to be more comfortable and prevent bedsores. The list goes on: a wheelchair, a bedpan towards the end…they were truly sympathetic listeners and gave us awesome support. They were angels!

If only there were more folks like them to go around, it would make other cancer patients feel a lot better, knowing there were people out there to listen and assist their loved ones through these terrible times.

Mom wanted to show her appreciation for these angels of mercy, so we bought them each a necklace for Christmas. That way they would always remember Mom and I. They 'oohed' and 'ahhed' and thanked us.

We couldn't begin to repay their kindness, no matter how many gifts we gave. We were so grateful for the dedication and compassion these individuals had for our family, in our time of need. I couldn't find the words to express how grateful I was for those angel volunteers.

The holidays passed and the New Year came. Mom was still at home with us. Hurray! I was doing something right. I spoke to the doctors to find out what Mom's status was and they said Mom wasn't going back to the hospital. There was nothing more they could do for her there. They told me that she should go to a nursing home. My heart was breaking.

The doctors explained Mom would get the best care there. The doctor was concerned I would have a nervous breakdown. Mom was getting sicker and sicker and it would be too much for me to handle her care at home.

Hospice agreed as well. The choice wasn't mine to make, and I couldn't begin to fight it. I prayed and prayed for an alternative. There simply wasn't one.

On January 7, 1981, on my twenty-eighth birthday, we had to move Mom into a nursing home. It was her last residence, so it appeared. I stayed to organize her room and to make it homey. She shared one room with other patients that were wheezing, coughing and "really" ill according to Mom. It was policy to have the patients together that took the same, or similar medication.

Mom didn't like this. I don't think Mom, for one minute, actually admitted that she, too, was really sick and dying. She never accepted defeat. A positive attitude is what kept her alive longer than the doctors predicted.

I have to admit, I was upset as well, so I spoke to one of the staff and requested Mom be moved to a different room by herself. It took some convincing but Mom did get moved. Now she had a colorful and pretty room. I got her a small television and brought her own pillow and comforter as well. I also brought her clothing, but mostly she wore pajamas and a robe.

It was difficult leaving her that first day. All I did was cry all the way home. I truly didn't want to leave my Mom again. I prayed for a miracle to have her come back home soon, but deep inside, I didn't believe it would happen.

Both of my sons would go with me to visit *Oma,* along with Kathy, whom I mentioned earlier. The boys were so young, I didn't expect them to understand how ill *Oma* was. They just loved on her and knew she lived at the big people's house.

Jesse was so proud of himself and was squirming excitedly to tell *Oma* of his latest achievement. The next time we went to see *Oma*, he said in his small voice, "*Oma, Oma,* I go peepee in the big toilet!"

Mom just showered him with hugs and kisses and told him what a big boy he was. When Mom was living at home, she patiently taught Jesse how to use the potty chair, so the achievement was super-duper to both of them.

Chris was Gramma's special grandchild, although she loved both of them equally. After all, she was at Chris's birth, and raised him, along with me, until Donald came into my life. She taught him so many good things, including how to draw and say his nightly prayers. In turn he taught his brother the same. Mom would spend hours and hours with Chris. So much love was there.

When we visited Mom at the "home," the kids liked to play and not actually sit still for any length of time. Mom understood. "Boys will be boys," she'd say.

One day, I went to see Mom and there was another patient in the bed next to her. I thought that was fine; Mom would have someone to talk to. Unfortunately, the lady found out Mom had cancer and wanted to be moved. I guess she thought cancer was catching or something. Not!

My Mother, Jesse, Chris - 1980

Mom had her own room again. I am sure it was lonely at night for her. As usual, she never complained. Mom met a person who had a room at the other end of the nursing home, who also had cancer. She and Mom were relatively young; all the rest of the patients were retirement age and above. Mom didn't tell me much, but I am sure the two of them reminisced and shared some beautiful and sad memories together.

A few weeks went by, then one weekend came and I told Donald I needed to see Mom alone, without the kids. I showered, cleaned up and put on a rather nice dress. I wanted a mom/daughter "fun" visit.

When I arrived at the home, I went to the soda machine and purchased a Pepsi for me and a Mountain Dew for Mom. At this point she good only tolerate liquids, and she loved that Mountain Dew taste.

I walked down the hallway, happy and looking forward to chatting with Mom, and I stopped near her doorway. It was dark inside her room. I slowly crept forward and saw the flicker of candlelight inside. That was when I saw her alive for the last time. Something was terribly wrong. Terrible thoughts went through my mind. Who had the answers?

Anna, a very good German friend of Mom's was by her bedside, praying. Anna and Mom met and became fast friends at one of Mom's treatments at the beginning of her illness. Anna saw me standing at the door and came to me, took the sodas from me and put them somewhere. Then she took my hands and said in broken English, "Your Mom's dying, Eve. Come sit down."

My heart was pounding so hard, I don't know why it didn't break out of my skin. I was confused. "What do you mean? My mom isn't dying. No! Not my Mom." Now I felt as if someone was pulling my heart apart. "It's not true," I cried.

Anna tried to pull me into the room. A part of me wanted so much to run to Mom's side and gather her up in my arms, and the other childlike part of me just wanted to run away and hide.

I couldn't do it, I just couldn't. I pulled my hand away from Anna and fled down the hallway to the nurses lounge, collapsed on the couch and broke down, sobbing my heart out.

I finally cried myself out and got up and went and found a phone to call Donald and tell him the horrible news. I explained that I couldn't bring the truck home, because I was not leaving Mom. He didn't know what to say except, 'I love you.'

After I hung up from Donald, I called Linda, a very close friend of mine. She said she would be down immediately to sit with me and pray for Mom's soul. I still wasn't ready to go into Mom's room, so I went back to the nurse's lounge and my mind was spinning. I don't have total recollection, because it was like I was existing in a fog. Everything I did was mechanical; I didn't feel "real."

A priest that spoke German was called in, but I'm not sure by whom. He spoke with me. I don't remember what he said to me. I am sure it was consoling words.

I thought I saw Donald walk by while I was speaking with the priest. Later I found out it was Donald; he had walked directly to my Mom's room to be with her. I needed Donald so badly and here he was.

Donald also brought his parents and sister Kay with him. What I couldn't grasp is why they brought my youngest son, Jesse, with them, but not Christopher. I loved both my sons endlessly, but at this moment, I didn't want either of my children there. I felt of the two, my seven-year-old, Chris, could have been there, but my three-year-old, Jesse, was plain too young to understand. Donald's family finally took Jesse back home.

Donald came and got me out of the nurse's lounge and took me to my Mom. The priest was there praying for Mom and we all held hands and prayed with him. I was finally was coming to reality. I prayed with all my might for release of pain for Mom and if that meant letting her go then so be it. I wanted her to have peace.

I knew she wasn't afraid. At one time she was afraid, but I think it was more because of the chemo and radiation, and fear for her family. As I stood next to her bed, I assured her, "We will be okay, Mom, and it is okay to let go."

It took every bit of bravery for me to say those words. I needed her so much. How could I go on without her?

It doesn't matter how young or old you are, it still wrenches you to lose a parent. I was going to be an orphan shortly.

I sat down beside her and took her hands, and told her how much I loved her. I said she was not only the best Mom, but the best *Oma* as well. I told her she would be forever in my heart and I would cherish her memory to the day I die.

I told her I would be the best mom in the world, because I had her as an example. I told her she was my one and only person that loved me unconditionally and never left me.

I kept repeating to her over and over again: "I love you Mom." "I love you Mom." "I love you Mom."

As I was holding her hand, I felt a slight squeeze, and Mom looked up at me and said in a whisper, "*Ich liebe dich fur die Ewgkeit mein kind.*" "I love you for all eternity my child."

Tears continued to roll down my very swollen eyes. I can't explain in words what I felt for Mom. She was truly my lifeline.

I looked at Mom's tiny shape under the blankets. She only weighed fifty-two pounds. She was a tough old gal though. She wanted more than anything for a miracle, to be able to stay alive and healthy for many more years. To see the boys grow, graduate, marry and maybe have some great-grandchildren to play with and love.

At a certain point, I had to accept that her time was fast approaching to go to the Lord. I didn't tell her I would be lost without her; I didn't tell her how desperately I would miss her. I didn't say, "Mom, I have no more family, because you were all the family I had until I made my own with Donald and my two children." I felt so alone. Empty.

I stayed in Mom's room for a bit longer, but then felt compelled to leave. I whispered, "Mother, darling, I do hope you can understand why I left your room." As much as I loved her, I was in so much pain and confusion. I thought I was losing my mind and myself, along with my mom.

Mom was supposed to get well; she was supposed to come home. Everything was happening in reverse. Images of abandonment from my childhood were racing through my mind, and the fear overwhelmed me.

I needed reassurance. I turned to God. I prayed. He was my solace, my parent, my protector. He helped me in the past to make it through. I could trust him now.

I knew Mom had nothing to be afraid of. She was going to her Heavenly Father forever. She would be home at last, to stay. I was so tired and had no sleep; all I did was cry. I was a mess, with swollen eyes and a stuffed up nose.

Finally I went back to the lounge, feeling very edgy and lightheaded. I laid down on the couch.

Donald, Linda, Kay, and Donald's parents went into to see Mom. My friend, Linda, told me that Donald walked up to the foot of Mom's bed and she looked up at her son-in-law and said to him, "Oh Donald."

I believe if she had more strength she would have said more to him. She just didn't have it in her anymore. She was so wasted away.

Linda said Mom looked like she was disappointed to see Donald's family there. It seemed like she was expressing "Why come now when I am dying, when you should have been around me at home, before this, and you weren't."

A lot of times people forget to visit the sick and provide them with what they need now, in life. Remember, our sick need to know they are still important to their friends and family, while they are alive. Ignoring a person during their bad times and illnesses, then attending their funeral is not what that person needs. They need you now, not later. Tell them you love them now, tell them they are a good friend now, and tell them they are a good parent now, because tomorrow may be too late.

One of the nurses came up to me and said that I should go home for awhile and get some rest. I didn't want to leave Mom, but Donald's mom and sister, Kay, promised to sit with Mom and reassured me she wouldn't be left alone. So I went home and couldn't sleep much. I was listening for the phone to ring for good news, not bad news, please.

I don't remember how long Donald's mom and sis stayed with Mom that night. A strange thing happened to me. I was lying in bed, and I looked over at the clock on the bed stand. It was 12:08 AM.

I felt a strange and wondrous peace inside myself. I finally fell asleep. At 3:00 AM, the phone rang and jarred me and Donald awake. I let it ring and ring and ring. I wasn't going to answer it. I knew what was going to be told to me. Finally, after about ten incessant rings I picked up the phone and uttered, "Hello."

A nurse who was sitting with Mom during the night, called to give me the chilling words I dreaded to hear, "Eve, I am so sorry, but your mother just passed away." Oh, the tears streamed heavily down my face. I don't think I ever cried so much in my life. And I have shed a lot of tears, believe me.

I asked so many questions. The nurse was sympathetic and answered as best she could. Would. Should. Did she have pain at the end? No. Did she say anything more? No. Were you there with her when she died? Yes. The nurse explained that Mom took one deep breath and went to sleep. That lightened my heart a bit. It was a peaceful passing for Mom. She deserved it.

My mom was only forty-eight years-old when she passed away. Her life was much too short, but oh, the impact she made on everyone who knew her

I believe I went into a kind of shock then. I vaguely realized she was gone, but what would I do without my mother? I sat at the kitchen table with the phone in my hand and numbly started calling everyone I knew to let them know that Mom was gone. I think I hoped some of the pain in my heart would recede. It didn't. The pain was so strong. I couldn't cry. I was in total despair.

The next morning, after a sleepless night, Donald and I had to go to the nursing home to pick up Mom's belongings. This was around 9:00 AM. It was one of the most difficult things I have ever done.

I picked up her robe, and it smelled like Mom. I buried my face in its soft folds and sobbed. Where was she? I missed her loving arms around me; her soft voice telling me everything would be okay. "Mom, Mom, my dearest, where are you? Please don't leave me all alone."

I later asked Rose and Kay why they left Mom alone to die. I also asked why they didn't call me to say they were leaving, so I could return to the hospital. I never got a response.

When Mom died, an ambulance picked her up and took her to the county. Then I went to Maricopa County Hospital to pick up Mom's rings and earrings. I think that's when I started feeling that it was really true. She was gone.

Donald had to work, so Kathy again went with me so I wasn't alone. I couldn't think straight, and everything was happening way too quickly. Kathy brought me home and I had to turn around and go to the funeral parlor to make the final arrangements. We didn't have much money, and Mom didn't have an insurance policy, because the cancer made her uninsurable. So unfortunately, Mom was buried in a particle board box. There were no satin covers in Mom's "box", only cotton draping her body. Donald was always there supporting my decisions.

When we returned later, we brought her favorite blue outfit Mom loved so much. Mom looked especially beautiful in blue. I couldn't get myself to agree to see her. I wanted to see her. I sat in the foyer of the funeral home and mentally fought with myself to step inside and go up to her casket, but I just couldn't.

I chose for her casket to remain closed, and I did get flack from other members of the family about my decision. I didn't care about other people's opinions. This was my Mom and solely my decision. Mom was so wasted away, it wasn't right to have her on display.

I saw her in life; I didn't want to see Mom in death. So I never did. I don't regret my decision. My mom was a beautiful woman and she wouldn't want to be seen in the state she was in. It was my last act of unselfish kindness for her.

I think it is a very personal decision to see someone in death, whether the person is a close relative or not. I know generally it is considered a closure for some. Frankly for me, I just wanted to remember Mom's vibrant and beautiful face, not lying still and painted up in a casket.

I felt bad that we didn't have the money to give her a better funeral, and felt guilty that I couldn't do more. This troubled me greatly. The answer came to me in a dream. The Lord said, "I brought your mother into this world without anything; I have taken her just the same. She doesn't need all the elaborate, material décor. She has me. That is all she needs."

I know her soul and the essence of her being is with the Lord, and that is all that matters. What helps me to survive with her passing, is knowing that one day I will see her again.

The funeral was in two days. They were terrible, two, long days to wait. Mom's burial day finally arrived. Donald and I decided to allow Chris to attend but not Jesse.

We felt he was too young and wouldn't understand all that was happening. Mom's casket was loaded up in the hearse and taken directly to the cemetery. There were no services at the funeral home. At the grave, all of our friends came and paid their respects. They were all so sweet and comforting.

The minister said a beautiful prayer, and I tearfully allowed the words to wash over me to give me peace. I don't remember any of the details of the service. I think I just floated through, making the motions that were expected of me.

Soon it was time to return home. Donald held me closely in his arms and assured me that he loved me dearly and how much he hurt for both of us. I knew he was going to miss Mom a lot as well.

I struggled within myself. I didn't want to leave her grave. I felt I couldn't go on without Mom. There was a tree by Mom's grave and I went over to it and held on tightly. I couldn't leave her. Donald finally convinced me. Donald, Chris and I got into our truck and started out for the long drive home; without Mom.

Over the next few weeks, we went through a lot of changes. There was no longer someone to hug and hold; no one to bring meds to; no one to talk to in German. There was a massive void.

Some part of me died along with Mom. I felt like part of my heart was empty and gone forever. To this day, I can still feel the emptiness. Sometimes, as I walk around, doing my daily chores, I sense Mom there beside me, helping me and guiding me. It is a comforting feeling.

I never gave up, because my two sons and husband gave me a reason to look at brighter things and face the future together. Most of all, I had my faith. God always carried me through the difficult times. He now had to carry me through this life without my Mom at my side.

Epilogue:

Thank you, Dear Readers, for walking through this part of my life with me.

My Mom went to her eternal rest without knowing the internal struggle I endured because of the rape. If my adopted father reads this book, he will find out I was raped at twelve years of age. I am a private person, but am convinced that my book will help someone.

Years have passed, but I hope and pray that if this happens to you, you tell someone right away.

We must all share and learn from one another's pain. It is a tragedy not to tell someone. Don't do like I did, carrying this horrific load alone for all these years. I spoke to the Lord, because I knew he wouldn't judge me and would lessen the pain I carried inside of me. I believe I have made it through this, because of His blessings. My resilience is part of my faith in Him.

Again, I stress, I am fortunate I didn't get pregnant, or worse, a disease. We who are raped, are the victims. We didn't ask for it, nor encourage it. It's the perverted mind that thinks they have the right to assault and rape an innocent, whether they are a boy or a girl. It's the sick mind that cannot take "no" for an answer and presses forward for their own evil pleasure.

For the men out there, be kind to the women in your lives. Treat them as if they were your mothers. They need understanding and protection. For the women out there, respect your bodies and don't tease the men. For the children out there, if anyone touches you inappropriately, tell your parents, your teachers, your counselors, or your minister. There is no reason to endure such behavior. No reason! Always cherish each other and listen to each other.

Adults have the power to hurt children, or to save children from disaster. Please, I beg you, when a child comes to you with pain and hurt in their eyes and tells you something horrible has happened to them, believe them. Be diligent in your efforts to prove or disprove what the child has stated. But, initially, all you should do is remove the child from the danger and put them in a safe haven, no matter how temporary. Then take the steps of proper notification to the appropriate authority.

Kids don't always make things up, especially when it comes down to sexual assault or rape. Don't be in denial, it happens every day in the "real" world and it could happen to your own. Frankly, Dear Readers, it will save that child from an everlasting world of hurt and negative effects of a lifetime. Some never recover to be mentally healthy from what has occurred in childhood.

***

Someday, I will ask my father why he didn't send my Mom and I back to Germany when he abandoned us. Yes, after almost forty years, I am in contact with him again. There are so many questions I have, and I hope someday he will give me the answers. The hurt in my heart is deep. My Dad not only left my Mom, but abandoned me during the most crucial time in my life, my childhood. I don't know why. What did I do wrong, to deserve his leaving me?

I have never once stated that my faith in God wasn't tested at times. It has been, and severely so. There are so many unanswered questions floating around in my head. There were times I was so overwhelmed, all I could do is cry. Mom always said, you had to have hope and faith each day for things to come the way they were supposed to be. I know those words have carried me through to the present. Through strife, misfortune, disappointments and terrible happenings, my faith has always been strong within me.

Many of us often wonder what we might have done, if we could do it all over again. That's what is funny about life, you only get one chance. It is impossible to do things over again, but you do learn how to get stronger and wiser from the conflicts you experience. You don't ever give up, no matter how deep or narrow your path seems at times. My mom had been through quite a few narrow and slim paths as you have seen. We never gave up in the face of adversity. We must always have faith that there is a better day to come. We must always have faith in God.

Dear Readers, always remember that whatever "face" you present to the world, your children can still "read" you. They are familiar with your happy face, and sad face, and angry face. Don't be fooled that children don't react to those dispositions. Kids are pretty darn smart. It leaves an impression on them as well. Your reaction to any given situation that they witness, will probably be theirs as well, when they experience the same, or similar situation. It's called imprinting.

My belief is that parents should be honest with their children, from the get-go. According to the child's age, give them limited information, that they can handle. As they get older, give them the details as needed. Reassure your children they are loved. Always present life altering events in a very positive light to the child.

Never, ever hide things. It will backlash on you later and affect your child adversely, if you evade the truth. It isn't easy to admit unusual circumstances, so perhaps you can consult a counselor or minister, or even a friend, that will advise you on the best approach to tell your child something. Just make sure you are honest, sincere and truthful.

Verbalize a "thank you," and let the people around you know that you appreciate them in your life. Tell them that you value them. You don't have to sound sappy about it, just express to them that they mean a lot to you. It will take you far in relationships of all types. Relationships are always a two way street, in good times and bad times. No matter what type of relationship, it has to be nurtured with love and acceptance.

Love for people is so wonderful to feel, because it is the one true emotion that God directed us to express. We need a Godly kind of love. We all have that gift. We just have to decide on how to utilize it. And that means anytime, anywhere, no matter how tough the road appears. Possessing material things is nothing, compared to having a person's love, respect, and admiration.

A lot of people take their lives for granted and don't enjoy the moment. Whether it is full of strife, or challenge, we learn from our experiences and our characters develop. If we had a soft life, it would be very boring, right? If the happy times are far and few between, take time to smell the roses. Mom and I certainly learned that the hard way. I lost my Mom early on in life and I wish every minute of my day I could have her back in my life, even for a moment. Each day we experience, is precious and cannot be repeated and we have no idea what will happen next.

Consider this: You are the last person left in the world. You now literally own everything left on this Earth; the cities, the lakes, the countries, the stock market, the food, and the animals. Everything. Does that make you feel happy and loved? I don't think so. Do you know why? Well, you are alone, without someone to share the wealth of the Earth with you. Our innate desires, placed in us by God, are for community, sharing and fellowship.

Yep. We need each other. You will feel so much peace, when you know you are right with God and right with those in your life and when you are loved. If only people in this crazy world would understand that most problems could be resolved amicably. So get on it, Dear Readers; tell someone how much you love them.

I hope this makes sense and reaches your soul. Thank you, for taking the time to walk through this book with me. I hope and pray, as you all have read this, that it has touched your hearts in a special way. Continue on with me in my second book, "The Journey We Call Life", soon to be published.

God Bless,

Evie

<u>Readers say:</u>

"Eve is genuine and inspiring. Her steadfast faith is a testimony to the grace of God and to the example her mother set for her: never, ever give up."
Debbi Migit
Author: *Child of Promise*
Editor: *What did I do wrong?*

"This inspirational book will open your eyes to a woman who has endured so much pain and sorrow and still remains positive in her daily life. We should all learn from her that life is too short not to forgive."
Timothy Sears

"It was difficult to take breaks in between reading and doing routine tasks. The title will catch a reader's attention and they will not be able to put it down."
Imogene Garlitz

"The fact that she never lost her faith in God kept my eyes peeled to the pages. Family is family and you do what you can for them to survive."
Christopher R. Slater

"You have an actual voice that comes out in writing. It is a voice that is extremely honest and sincere. You say it how it is and how you felt."
Eve's Nutritionist

"This book was an inspirational story of one woman's will to keep going. Don't take anyone for granted, you might not have the chance to repair the damage."
Eve's Physician's Nurse

"It takes you through a journey of persistence and perseverance. It inspires others to keep pushing forward and to think twice before giving up."
Behavioral Health Consultant

"I learned from this book that no matter what happens I have to continue to do my best in life."
Alfonso Zargoza

"Some women have gone through the same things, and as women can relate to her and understand."
Church Member

"My question has been, how does Eve maintain such a positive, innocent outlook on life despite all her sorrows? It has to be the gift of unshakeable faith that has guided her in life. She is pure of spirit. I have been blessed by her friendship."
Maryann Germain

"The lines you wrote about people are brought into our paths for a specific reason and a season helped me. Earlier this year, a couple my husband and I know who we have been friends with for 10 years and did many, many things with, all of a sudden do not want to associate with us any longer. I still don't know what happened. I had been feeling really low about it, and when I read the lines in your book, it did help me to kind of understand that whatever did happen, we probably had no control over and to basically let it go. We have met so many wonderful people in this little community that I can go on and not think about it so much."
Carol

"I got your book and really enjoyed reading about all your experiences. You sure did persevere well, didn't you? God helped bring you through a lot and now you are finally enjoying the fruits of your labors all those years. It is said that if we endure well, we will enjoy as much joy in later life as we did pain in the earlier years.......and I have happily found it to be so...so far! God bless you as you continue in His way with your family and writing the next two books in that series."
Barbara Ashley

"If asked what the book did for me, I would have to say that it so much confirmed that we are not alone in our sufferings in this world.....many women struggle and grow stronger as a result. Your story was especially interesting to me because you lived through much of the same time period that I did. I found that very interesting. I also related very much to your deep loyalty and love for your mother. Mine died on May 31st of this year and I know that I will miss her deeply for the rest of my days on this earth. I so much look forward to being reunited with her one day. I'm glad you are continuing to tell your story...so many women need to hear about the God who rescued us and set us on higher ground! Thank you for sharing your life!"
Blessings,
Leslie

"I have finished your book. It took me a day and a half. What I can tell you is that you have been through a lot, but God was always there with you. Your story is an inspiration to many people. I lost my father when I was 3; he was murdered. I did not get to know him. I was raised by a single mother until I was 12. My step-father was wonderful. Although I had gone to church, I never knew Jesus for **real** until 2008. He has touched my life in so many ways. No matter what happens don't ever lose track of your real father Jesus."
Cindy Craig

"I downloaded it (the book) from Barnes and Noble and got through two chapters last night. You've done a wonderful job of keeping the reader interested! I have a busy day, but look forward to getting back to your book this evening. I find it interesting that my stepfather was in the army and has two sons from a marriage who live there. I've had the blessing of communicating with them by e-mail since his passing in 2007. My husband's family is German but has lived in the US for a long time. I visualize that the book I would like to write would encourage a Christian mother like yours...a beautiful woman of faith who found herself in challenging and dark times. It's inspirational for me to know that you wrote your story. I'm needing to focus now on mine. Thank you for being faithful to our Lord. Thank you for being a blessing to women!"
Leslie Shaw Holzmann
http://journeytodignity.com

"My heart is filled with joy. I see God at work and what He brought to you He will bring you through it. This has to have given you a special lift as I'm sure it is a confirmation that you are obeying God and ready to be used in a greater way. Keep in touch Evie as you are special."
Curt Siegfried

"I could NOT put it (your book) down and finished it early this morning. It was to ironic to read about your bumpy road threw life. And the reason I choose the word "ironic" is in many parts of your story I felt as though I can relate. I was reading the chapter about how you were raped. For starters, I am very sorry to have read that. That is NO pain that anyone should endure. But I can relevantly relate to that, because my mother was a rape victim. I wasn't aware of that until less than a year ago, and it the term I found out I have a younger brother whom my mother had given up for obvious reasons. We met and have grown a great bond as brothers in the short time that we have known one another."

"Also through the majority of your book, you talk about how you and your mother had such a great bond. I understand that also, my mother was my best friend for most of my life, and probably still is to this day. And also with the stories of your dad. I also found out my father wasn't really my father about the age of 13 or 14. And since I have had children of my own, he's come to a point were it seems as thought he wants nothing to do with me. All threw the book there were a lot of close relations I had and was able to understand threw the eyes of a "victim". But to keep this short and simple. I was telling my wife about these very events that I had mentioned in this letter, she was in awe. I am eagerly awaiting for "The Journey We Call Life" to be realized."
Bubba Lara.

"After reading "What Did I Do Wrong" it made me realize just how easy we all have it today. Evie is a very strong women whom I have a lot of admiration for. Trust in the "Lord", and you shall receive."
Bonnie Wells

"We always go through trials in our life and lose hope. Your book made me feel Love and hope with each word. You turned darkness to light and light to belief. Not only could I get a mental image of your story, but I could feel it in my heart. Many thanks for sharing your life with me. You gave me much hope where there wasn't any. Enjoyed your book; very touching. Can't wait for the second one."
Donna

"I loved your book, it is a page turner; you do not want to put it down. I felt your pain and hardships throughout your story. I can relate to a lot of it. I have lived with a lot of hardships too, as I've told you most of my story. God Bless You and keep you strong. Glad you found love at last. I sat and read this in one setting. LOL Was very hard to put down. Got it read in one night."
Dawn

"Amazing Story! My heart goes out to you Evie. You are the most courageous women I have ever met. Your mom is always with you on earth or in Heaven. You are a beautiful angel. The book brought tears to my eyes. Such a beautiful story."
Judy Stoffel

"Our entire staff was blown-away by this book. It is one of the most inspiring inspirational books I have ever read. Eve has had quite the life story. Perhaps the question she should ask herself is "What did I do right?" She must have done something right just in order to have survived. Most people that had endured what she had, would have spent their time complaining about how unfair life had treated them and not attempted to make things better. Eve has thrived."

"Many others would spend their time blaming God for their troubles, whereas her faith has only grown stronger. She is to be congratulated on becoming the person she has, and sharing her story with all those that would read it. It truly puts into perspective all of the problems that we all deal with on a daily basis..."
Richard S. Hartmetz
CEO - Starry Night Publishing

Eveline Sandy

About the Author:

Eveline Gabriel Darlene Behm Ramos Sandy was born in Germany. Her dream has been to be able to write this book for all of you to learn something in your own life through what she has lived. Eve and her husband, Donald, have two sons, Christopher and Jesse. They also share their love with their grandsons: Christopher, 15; Jesse Jr., 12; Donald, 8; and Jeremy, 3.
Eve and her family reside in Mayer, Arizona.

To contact Eve Sandy………<sweetoma@msn.com>

Eveline Sandy

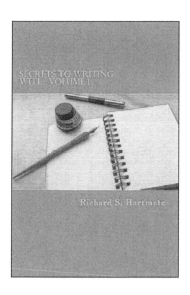

I'm going to put it bluntly. Not every author who writes well gets published and not every author who gets published writes well. I am going to try and help you write well and hopefully get published too.

As Charles Dickens once wrote: "There are books of which the backs and covers are by far the best parts."

We are going to look first at the elements that go into writing a fictional story; what they are, how to use them effectively and how to put them together to make a good story. We are going to start with a basic story and work on developing it together so you can observe the actual process. Then you can feel free to go off an do one on your own.

This volume will cover Setting, Point of View, Tense, Mood, Plot Types, Dialogue and Character Development. It is written by Richard S. Hartmetz, who has had more than a dozen books published and is the CEO of Starry Night Publishing. Richard is a long-time teacher of writing workshops.

Secrets to Writing Well - Volume 1

Eveline Sandy

OUR VISION

Our goal is to help you get your story into print. It really is that simple.

As authors ourselves, we understand the frustration of repeated rejections from the big publishing companies and the elitist agents. It becomes a Catch 22 when you have to be a big name in order to get published and become a big name. We're here to eliminate that step and the potential heartbreak that accompanies it and put the power back in your hands.

We are not a "vanity publisher" who charges you as much as $8,000 to receive a handful of substandard paperbacks, just so you can hand them out to the relatives at Christmas and never sell another copy. We get you published and marketed both in paperback and e-book format on Amazon.com and other major online retailers. We also don't charge to get you published, we only charge a small fee for preparing your book.

You earn up to a 60% royalty rate with us, instead of the typical 10% that the traditional publishing houses pay. Why should you do all the work and allow them to keep 90% of your profit? And the best part is, you retain 100% of the rights to your work!

THE FUTURE IS NOW!

Gone are the days when an author would sit in front of an old manual typewriter, rubbing holes in the paper or filling their office garbage cans with unsalvageable scrap. The publishing industry is evolving. The old publishing houses are becoming dinosaurs. E-books are everywhere. They are cheaper than old-fashioned books, use less paper and ink, faster to produce, take up less space and can be read on any computer, e-reader or Smartphone.

Success comes to those who make opportunities happen, not those who wait for opportunities to happen. You can be successful too, you just have to try...

A recent poll suggested that nearly 85% of parents would encourage their child to read a book on an e-reader. More than 1 in 5 of us owns an e-reading device and the number is climbing rapidly. For every 100 hardcover books that Amazon sells, it sells 143 e-books. They also never go out of print!

Hundreds of thousands of independent authors, just like you, are selling their profitable work as you read this. E-book sales have grown over 200% in the past year and account for more than $1 billion in annual sales.

Chances are, you don't even know the difference between a PDF, mobi, ePub, doc, azw, or the fifteen other competing formats struggling to coexist on the sixteen types of e-reader devices such as the Kindle or the Nook. Even if you are able to keep up with all the devices and their formats, do you want to spend the money for expensive software to convert your files, or the many hours it will take to figure out how it works? Will you be able to create an interactive table of contents?

Our editors are professionals with experience in computer science, graphic design and publishing. We can do the work or you, creating a top-notch book that you will be proud of. Of course, you still have to write it, but that's the fun part...

BE A PART OF OUR COMMUNITY

Reach your intended audience in the worldwide marketplace by distributing your work on Amazon, Barnes and Noble and other major online booksellers. Earn royalties, get feedback, Join the discussions in the forum and meet other people in our community who share the same interests you do.

We will publish your fiction or non-fiction books about just about anything, including poetry, education, gardening, health, history, humor, law, medicine, pets, philosophy, political science, psychology, music, science, self-help travel, science-fiction, fantasy, mystery, thriller, children and young adult, etc....

http://www.starrynightpublishing.com

Made in the USA
San Bernardino, CA
04 April 2015